Tucker Boyd tore his eyes off of Casey long ___ ___ to throw his coach a look of curiosity. "What's up, ___ ___rdo? I thought you had a meeting with the Baseball Prince ___ this morning."

Gordon's eyes flickered from Tucker to Casey, **then back to** Tucker again, a look of alarm spreading across his ruddy features. "Boyd, I wouldn't—"

"Don't worry about it, Gordon," Casey interrupted, her voice cool and even. "We're considering putting Boyd on the team because of his arm, not his manners."

As Tucker's jaw dropped even further, Casey strode reagally past. She gave him one final, level stare. "By the way, don't throw the ball too hard. You've got several weeks of spring training to go, you know. Warm up slowly. There's no point in risking your recovery."

Boyd's expression was grim, all traces of laughter gone. "Don't you worry about my arm."

Casey nodded at him and made a hasty exit, her heart beating out

Ou ___ r the

beauti ___ nted

on h

813.54 Mac   9063
MacDonald, Shari.
Diamonds

BL: Pts: Q#

Adventure Christia___
6401 Stanford ___
Roseville, C
(916) 771

D0731587

PALISADES...PURE ROMANCE

Palisades.
Pure Romance.

FICTION THAT FEATURES CREDIBLE CHARACTERS AND
ENTERTAINING PLOT LINES, WHILE CONTINUING TO UPHOLD
STRONG CHRISTIAN VALUES. FROM HIGH ADVENTURE
TO TENDER STORIES OF THE HEART, EACH PALISADES
ROMANCE IS AN UNDILUTED STORY OF LOVE,
FROM BEGINNING TO END!

THERE IS NO SUCH TEAM AS THE BEND BACHELORS, nor is there a franchise called the Phoenix Stars. However, after the Rockies baseball team moved to Portland, Oregon, in 1994, Bend, Oregon, did become home to a new single-A team known as the Bend Bandits. The Bandits and the fictional Bachelors share a hometown, but all similarities end there.

I am indebted to Dan DiLella of the Bend Bandits for valuable bits of information which contributed to the development of *Diamonds*. However, nothing in this story should be interpreted as a representation of the Bandits, their management, players, or league.

A PALISADES CONTEMPORARY ROMANCE

DIAMONDS

SHARI MACDONALD

PALISADES

This is a work of fiction. The characters, incidents, and dialogues are products of the author's imagination and are not to be construed as real. Any resemblance to actual events or persons, living or dead, is entirely coincidental.

DIAMONDS
published by Palisades
a part of the Questar publishing family

© 1996 by Shari MacDonald
International Standard Book Number: 0-88070-982-0

Cover illustration by George Angelini
Cover designed by Mona Weir-Daly
Edited by Judith Markham

Printed in the United States of America

ALL RIGHTS RESERVED
No part of this publication may be reproduced, stored in a retrieval system, or transmitted, in any form or by any means—electronic, mechanical, photocopying, recording, or otherwise—without prior written permission.

For information:
QUESTAR PUBLISHERS, INC.
POST OFFICE BOX 1720
SISTERS, OREGON 97759

96 97 98 99 00 01 02 03 04 — 10 9 8 7 6 5 4 3 2 1

SPECIAL THANKS...
To my beloved Craig,
for all your love, patience, understanding, and prayers.
(And for helping me dream up Barry Bachelor.)

To my sister, Debbie Peterson,
for slaving over the book with me and for helping
me keep (more or less) my sanity.

To Bruce DeRoos,
for coming up with the idea of a baseball romance and for
blathering on endlessly about your love for the game.
(Now stop it.)

To Steve Olson and Steve Spotts, for making sure I sounded
like I knew what I was talking about.

To Dan DiLella, promo manager for the Bend Bandits,
for giving me tips about minor league promotions and for offering to be the book's main character, if it needed one.

To Mom and Dad, Dan, Isaac, Naomi, Mark, Ryan, Liz,
Lindy, Sarah, Claire, Susan, Robin, and all my other loved ones
who had to put up with me disappearing for weeks in order to
get my work done. You're the best.

AND MOST OF ALL...
To God,
for keeping me afloat when I got in over my head,
and for helping me fulfill more responsibilities than I thought
was humanly possible without having a nervous breakdown.

"All things are possible through Christ, who strengthens me...."
PHILIPPIANS 4:13

To the one who started it all…
Lisa Tawn Bergren,
my managing editor, coworker, cheerleader, and friend.
Thanks for asking,
"Hey, do you want to write a romance?"

I see great things in baseball....
WALT WHITMAN, 1846

MONDAY, FEBRUARY 17—PHOENIX, ARIZONA

asey Foster stepped up to home plate and inhaled deeply of the thin Arizona air. As always, the sight of the diamond gave her a rush, and the familiar surge of adrenaline made her fingers itch for her battered Rawlings mitt. She hadn't played ball competitively since her senior year at college, but four years later the game was still a part of Casey's soul.

Bright sapphire eyes opened wide as she surveyed the scene before her. One of four practice fields at the training complex of the new Phoenix Stars, the stretch of grass was flawlessly manicured and ready for play. Casey's lips twitched in amusement. She hoped her players wouldn't get used to such luxurious conditions. They were guests here—poor relation guests at that. A working agreement between the teams allowed her double-A Bend Bachelors to share spring training facilities with the new major league franchise. But spring training would end before too long. Meanwhile, back home, a typical minor league ballpark awaited, with rain-blistered bleachers, a bumpy outfield...and a lush green diamond more beautiful than any jewel Casey had ever seen.

A smile played upon her lips at the recollection. Two weeks earlier she had seen her team's field for the first time. Minor league ballparks were notorious for being run-down and ill-equipped, so Casey had expected the worst. Yet, despite its shortcomings, the outdoor stadium was wonderfully endearing; she found it authentic and unspoiled, unlike the temperature-controlled arenas in which she had spent so many hours of her career as a struggling sportscaster. And quite unlike the triumph of sports architecture now stretched out before her under a cloudless Arizona sky. With its five indoor batting cages and pitching areas, four practice fields, state-of-the-art clubhouses and offices, and a seven-thousand-seat stadium, Star City's thirty-million-dollar complex was the envy of every major league franchise in the nation.

"Uncle Edward certainly knew what he was doing when he made a deal with the Stars," Casey muttered under her breath. An avid baseball fan and wealthy business tycoon, Edward Foster had decided two years earlier, at the age of fifty-eight, that it was time to turn his attention from his second greatest interest, wine-making—an enterprise which had made him one of the wealthiest business owners on the West Coast—to his number one passion, baseball. After learning of the upcoming addition of a Phoenix-based expansion team to the National League, Foster had worked out a deal that allowed him to establish a double-A farm team for the new franchise.

Transitions on the West Coast over the past few years had opened up a tremendous window of opportunity. With the defection of the Portland Beavers to Salt Lake City, Oregon's small-town Bend Rockies had moved to the state's biggest city to meet the needs of the sports-hungry Portland market. The void left in Central Oregon was one Casey's uncle had been happy to fill, especially since it was conveniently located due north of his Napa Valley home. The appropriate meetings were scheduled. The ballpark was leased. Contracts with the Phoenix Stars management were signed. Edward Foster was on his way to making his dream come true.

Throughout the planning stages, Casey had been her uncle's greatest supporter and most trusted confidante. From the beginning, she had helped him with his most difficult decisions—from general business operations to choosing a coaching staff to inviting talent to spring training.

"Good thing I have you, my brilliant sportscaster niece, to get me the inside scoop on all the players," he'd teased.

"Good thing I have you, my brilliant mastermind uncle, to tell me everything I know about the game!" she'd returned with a laugh.

Casey adored her Uncle Edward. It wasn't difficult to do. She and her brother, Aaron, had been essentially fatherless from the time they were toddlers. Although their father had abandoned his family, for a few years Douglas Foster showed up every six months or so to take Casey and her brother out to a Dodgers or Angels game. Then he would disappear as quickly as he had come, and Casey would settle back into her childhood dreams of playing a baseball game good enough to make her father want to stay.

Despite Casey's childhood wishes that her father would come to watch her Little League games, Douglas Foster had never shown up. But his brother, Uncle Edward, had. Countless times he had appeared in the stands at her Little League games—mumbling excuses about being in town on business—to cheer Casey on.

By the time Casey was six, Uncle Edward had begun making regular weekend visits to their Whittier, California, home, flying down from northern California to spend weekends entertaining his only niece and nephew. Their mother, still young, beautiful, and socially active, was grateful for the freedom this gave her to be involved in various clubs and activities. Casey and Aaron benefited as well. Although their dad disappeared for the last time when Casey was fourteen, Uncle Edward continued to come for regular visits. Casey and her brother were thrilled to have a loving father figure in their lives. For his part, Edward simply stated that he enjoyed the children's company and couldn't love them any more if they were his own.

The feeling was mutual. Casey could not have loved him more. Thus, after her uncle's death four months ago, she had found herself once again lonely and shaken, abandoned by the man she had loved most in the world—*and* the owner of a minor league ball team.

Casey's thoughts drifted back to the makeshift practice diamond she and the neighbor kids had forged from an abandoned lot. Filthy, exhausted, covered with scrapes and bruises, they would compete long into the summer nights…until darkness swallowed up even routine ground balls and long-suffering mothers descended upon the field to drag their wayward children home. *That's the mark of real baseball,* Casey thought, her love for sandlot ball still coloring her view of the game. *When you can walk into the park at night and see the stars.*

She blinked at the sky, growing brighter with the rising sun. No chance of seeing any stars from the field at this time of day. She glanced at her watch: 7:21 A.M. *Ugh.* As an up-and-coming sportscaster for a B-market television station in San Francisco, Casey had spent the past few years settling into a routine of late-night broadcasts and slumber-filled mornings. Her alarm never rang before 9:00 A.M., and rarely did she start her day without a cup of her favorite Sulawesi-blend coffee, the only brew she'd found strong enough to bring her to life before noon.

She wished she'd taken the time to stop for a cup this morning. Nervous about her meeting with the coaches of her newly acquired team, Casey had been lucky to get out of her hotel room with her hair parted properly and two matching shoes on her feet. She glanced down at her outfit. Not bad, considering the hour. The decision to wear black—her best color—had been a wise one. In a fitted, three-button jacket and pleated, tapered-leg trousers, she knew she looked sleek and trim. One slim hand flew to her thick auburn hair; thanks to the heavy new gel she was using, it was holding its contemporary chin-length style, rather than springing off into its customary fly-away waves.

Glancing at her feet, she noticed that little bits of mud had attached themselves to the sides and soles of her best stacked-heel mules. Casey groaned, wishing she'd worn her cheap flats to the field, as was her practice when conducting interviews. Then she remembered the purpose of her visit to the training facilities: She was the new owner of Bend's new double-A team. Although she would have preferred to wear her sloppiest sweats, she had an image to present, and neither her favorite Keds nor imitation-leather flats would do. She only hoped that the confidence she projected outwardly might camouflage her true feelings of uncertainty.

Impulsively, she decided to take a quick walk around the perimeter of the field to clear her head. She started out toward the far left field corner, dragging her hand along the rough Cyclone fence that paralleled the third base foul line.

It felt good to be on a ball field again, and Casey itched to drink in the effect from a better vantage point. She set out at a quick trot. Her meeting inside the clubhouse was due to start soon. Still, she followed her inner urging and headed toward the hard cloth-covered bag that was second base, hoping that a few moments at center field might settle her thoughts and calm her jangled nerves.

She was halfway across the field when her attention was

caught by the familiar thud of baseballs hitting dirt. Casey spun around just in time to see a tall figure leaning over the pitcher's mound, the contents of a large nylon sports bag spilling out and rolling about his feet.

Her heart sank at the sight of him: six-foot-two, muscular and tan, dark brown hair, with a square jaw…and he was standing on the pitcher's mound. There was no mistaking Tucker Boyd. Once people met "Big Time" Boyd, they never forgot him. Casey knew she never would.

A faint throbbing began to pulse at her temple, and her stomach muscles tightened as she remembered the last time she had seen Boyd. It was during her first year as a sportscaster. Young and eager, she had jumped at the chance to fill in for the regular announcer at her company's A-market sister station in Seattle. She was particularly excited about meeting Boyd. She'd seen him play before, and she liked the way he interacted with the kids who watched from behind the fence, near the dugout. He always had time for them, Casey noticed, and often he called the children by their names.

He didn't sign any autographs after this game, however. After Boyd's team suffered a crushing defeat by the hometown Mariners, Casey joined the other reporters in the locker room, hoping to get an interview—or at least a decent quote. She couldn't believe her luck when Boyd's eyes met hers across the crowd and he actually waved for her to ask a question.

Casey had cleared her throat and asked boldly: "Mr. Boyd, do you, in any way, blame tonight's loss on your unusually poor pitching?"

Boyd's eyebrows furrowed slightly. He spent what felt like several minutes—but was probably merely seconds—studying Casey from head to toe. Then, apparently having decided that she was worth an answer, he replied: "I couldn't say, really. There are a lot of variables." He shrugged, but somehow it didn't seem like a casual gesture. "Anyway, it doesn't matter a whole lot *how* I played. It takes good pitching to win a ball game. But it takes runs, too. And we didn't score a single run." He took a deep breath. "I'm not trying to shift the blame. I'm including myself in that criticism. I didn't hit better than anyone else tonight. We were all out of sync. I just don't think you can blame a loss on any one factor."

Casey hesitated, trying to decide whether to pursue that line of questioning. But before she could continue, the reporter next to her, a weasely looking man with heavy tortoiseshell glasses, took up where she left off.

"But you let the *Mariners* score. *Several* times." The Seattle reporter tried his best to conceal a smile, but he could not keep the corners of his mouth from turning up at the corners.

Boyd planted two fists on his jean-clan hips and narrowed his gaze. "I didn't *let* anybody do anything."

"But you are responsible for those runs being scored," the man persisted.

Boyd was silent for a moment. Then, "What's your point?" he asked levelly.

The reporter shrugged. "Just that pitching *does* figure into any loss. Don't you agree?"

A hush had descended upon the locker room as, one by one, Boyd's teammates took notice of the exchange. Casey watched, alarmed, as a couple of them went to stand beside Boyd. At first she imagined that they intended to help their star player start a fight. But then, as she noticed the nervous looks they were throwing Tucker—and each other—she realized they were actually worried about stopping one.

The visiting pitcher stepped menacingly toward the reporter, then stopped himself as second baseman Davy Ovitz laid a firm hand on his shoulder. "I *hate* to lose," Boyd ground out between clenched teeth. "This was *not* my fault."

17

The reporter shrugged again. "Whatever you say," he said with an innocent smile.

Boyd's face turned bright red, and he looked ready to pounce on the smaller man, who was obviously trying to bait the pitcher into giving him a colorful quote. Without thinking, Casey opened her mouth and entered the fray.

"Of course it wasn't your fault," she said brightly, hoping to somehow smooth things over. "You obviously did the best you could."

Tucker shifted his gaze to Casey, then back again to the weaselly reporter. He seemed to be trying to determine whether the two were together. Casey took a small side step, as though to distance herself from the troublemaker.

"What is that supposed to mean?" Boyd asked angrily.

"I—Nothing!" Casey sputtered, flustered by the sudden attack. She felt her face grow scarlet as every eye in the room turned upon her. At her side, the snide reporter let out a sharp, nasally laugh that seemed to push Boyd over the edge.

"All right, all right...who let these two amateurs in the locker room?" he said, glancing around, looking for someone in charge. "Somebody get them out of here."

"Hey! I'm not an amateur!" Casey protested hotly, anger finally getting the better of her. "What's the matter with you anyway? Okay, so you're mad that you lost. Big deal. Don't take it out on us. There's no need to be nasty, no matter how stupid a person's questions may be." She glared at the man beside her, then turned back to her attacker. "You don't have to be so defensive, you know. It's only a game!"

As soon as the words were out of her mouth, Casey knew she had made a mistake. In her days as a college player, she would have been deeply offended by such a statement—particularly right after a defeat like the one Boyd's team had just suffered. It only made it worse that she was surrounded by a roomful of men—both players and reporters—who had made professional sports the focal point of their lives. She could see from their expressions that her choice of words had done nothing to raise their opinion of her. Tucker Boyd, in particular, seemed to take her statement as a personal affront.

"Just a game? *Just* a game? Excuse me," he said acidly, "but how did you get to be a sports reporter anyway?" He glanced around again, as if looking for someone to escort her from the locker room. When no manager appeared, Casey worried for a moment that Boyd might throw her unceremoniously over one shoulder and remove her from the premises himself.

"I'm sorry—" she tried weakly, but Boyd would have none of it.

He turned away with a disgusted sigh. "Look, let's just forget about it, all right?" The men around him looked relieved, and the crowd began to disperse as the players stepped back toward their lockers and the reporters resumed their interviews. Casey looked around for the man who had instigated the conflict, hoping to shift the blame back to where it belonged, but he seemed to have vanished completely.

She made her way through the crowd to where Boyd was rummaging through his locker. "Umm, excuse me. I really *am* sorry. Do you think we could start over?" she said, speaking to the back of Boyd's T-shirt. For a moment the pitcher paused, as if considering her request. Then he turned and looked directly into her eyes, his expression softening slightly. As she waited for his response, it struck Casey, crazily, that Tucker Boyd had the most incredible hazel eyes she had ever seen: rich, honey-colored irises marked by little flecks of gold, surrounded by a slightly darker ring of…

"No. I don't think so," Boyd's booming voice interrupted her detailed study of his features. Casey blinked at the sound and tried to refocus. He didn't think—what? What had she asked?

Boyd looked a little sad, but he turned away just the same. "You probably mean well. You look like a nice girl." Normally, Casey bristled at being called a "girl." In the male-dominated fields of sports and sportscasting, she had enough gender biases to deal with; the last thing she needed was to be perceived as a college coed. But the sting of Boyd's dismissal demanded her entire focus. She watched as he continued rummaging through his locker and pulled out a deodorant stick. Then he turned to face her once again. "I just don't see how you could conduct a credible interview. You obviously don't understand the importance of the game." His explanation was gentle, yet firm.

"But I—" She stopped at the look Boyd gave her. He stood, with antiperspirant poised midair, clearly waiting for her to leave so he could finish his grooming. Casey considered pushing the argument, but it was obvious that the damage had been done. As much as she dreaded facing her editor without the interview, she knew it was time for her to leave the clubhouse. No one would be willing to talk with her now. And she couldn't really blame them.

Two years later, Casey still smarted from the humiliation of that incident. And now she was faced with Tucker Boyd again, even though she'd anticipated that such a day might come. When her uncle first mentioned that the Stars were interested in Boyd, Casey had shuddered, but assumed that any connection would be distant at best. But after last year's mid-season shoulder injury caused Boyd to be dropped from his team's roster, the up-and-coming superstar was invited to the Phoenix training camp, where he would have an opportunity to prove that his healing was complete—and his arm ready.

Although spring training did not officially start until mid-February, pitchers and catchers commonly began training before the rest of the prospects. It was likely that he had been in town for at least two weeks.

Casey looked at him, thinking, *Practice doesn't start until ten. No player ever gets here before nine. Why did he have to show up now?*

She stared at Tucker's back as he finished his warm-up tosses and wound up his long muscular arm to throw a fastball.

I'll bet he was thrilled to find out who his new boss will be. A soft laugh escaped her lips, and Casey clamped one hand over her mouth as Boyd let go a wild pitch.

Muttering angrily under his breath at his break in concentration, Boyd spat on the dirt and turned to identify the source of the sound. At the sight of Casey, he straightened and regarded her with surprise.

"Uh, miss…could you—" He looked momentarily uncertain as to what to do. "That is, I'm practicing my pitching, and it would be easier if you weren't on the field." He flashed her a pro-ball media smile. "But I hate to be rude to a fan. I tell you what. I need to concentrate for a while, and that's hard to do with you back there distracting me. Come back in an hour or so, and I'll spring for a cup of coffee. How's that? Do we have a deal?"

Casey blinked at him for a moment, then understanding dawned on her. He didn't know who she was! But he was used to being the focus of attention—both from the media and from fans. *Especially women,* Casey thought wryly, considering Boyd's good looks. *That's it! He thinks I'm a groupie, out here to hang on his every move…or beg for a lock of his hair.* Laughter threatened to surface once more, but this time she managed to control herself. *The nerve! The ego!*

Before she had stopped to think, Casey opened her mouth and heard herself saying, "Well, that's just fine. I'll get going now and let you practice with an empty stadium." She smiled at him innocently. "That will be good experience for the next time you find yourself competing with no one at bat, no runners on base, and no players in the field."

At the sound of her words, something about Boyd changed. The look of benevolent indulgence was replaced by an expression of mild irritation. He remained speechless, but his unspoken question was clearly written on his face: *Don't I know you from somewhere?*

It was sweet revenge, but Casey had little time to savor the victory. As Boyd stared at her, the Bachelors' batting coach, Gordy Olson, stepped onto the field and waved her toward the clubhouse.

Tucker tore his eyes off of Casey long enough to throw the coach a look of curiosity. "What's up, Gordo? I thought you had a meeting with the Baseball Princess this morning."

Olson's eyes flickered from Tucker to Casey, then back to Tucker again, a look of alarm spreading across his ruddy features. "Boyd, I wouldn't—"

"Don't worry about it, Gordon," Casey interrupted, her voice cool and even. "We're considering putting Boyd on the team because of his arm, not his manners."

As Tucker's jaw dropped even further, Casey strode regally past.

"Wait a minute. You're Gordon's new boss? And you say *you're* considering *me*? Don't make me laugh!" Boyd stared at Casey, and the look of intensity on his face told her that laughing was the furthest thing from his mind. "I'm not going down to the minors. When the season opens, I'll be back in the show, pitching for the Stars," he insisted.

Her poise recovered, Casey stopped and turned to face him. "Well, I guess that's up to the Stars, now, isn't it?" she said pointedly. She gave him one final, level stare. "By the way, don't throw the ball too hard. You've got several weeks of spring training to go, you know. Warm up slowly. There's no point in risking your recovery."

Boyd's expression was grim, all traces of laughter gone. "Don't you worry about my arm."

Casey nodded at him and made a hasty exit, her heart beating out a staccato rhythm in her chest.

Out on the pitcher's mound, Tucker Boyd stared after the beautiful brunette for several minutes, her image still imprinted on his mind long after she had disappeared.

All I ask is that you respect me as a human being.

JACKIE ROBINSON, FIRST BLACK PLAYER IN THE MAJOR LEAGUES

Thanks for taking the time to meet with me, gentlemen." As Casey smiled graciously, four sets of eyes peered warily back at her from around the formica table. "I know you're very busy."

"Yeah, we are," a deep voice interjected. Casey turned toward her pitching coach, Don Shelton, at her right. "But you're the boss now, aren't ya?" The heavyset man spoke casually enough, but Casey suspected that he was aiming his words carefully. "It's not like we could say no, now, is it?"

She took a deep breath. It was starting, just as she had known it would.

During her career as a sports reporter, Casey had learned that women were rarely welcomed with open arms into the world of male-dominated sports. Cheerleaders were accommodated—with a wink and a nod. Female sportscasters were tolerated—barely. But women owners and coaches were another story altogether.

As she'd listened to disparaging locker-room comments about "the old witch" or "Big Mama," Casey had always pitied the women who held positions of authority over these men.

24

Although there were already a number of highly capable women in the field of professional baseball—and countless others with ability, should they be willing to enter the fray—Casey knew that the battle for respect these women waged was long and hard fought.

There was little Casey could do to change the situation, although she did what she could to help. Whenever possible, she mentioned these women's contributions during her broadcasts. On a personal basis, Casey used her charm—and growing popularity among the players—to challenge such comments, and she had actually gotten a few of the men to retract their insults. Although most single ballplayers still approached her as a potential romantic conquest and the married players treated her like a little sister, Casey had finally begun to earn a measure of professional respect—despite her "college coed" appearance...and her big mouth.

The latter she now struggled to keep under control as she faced the circle of faces around the table.

Directly to her left sat the man Casey considered her closest ally in the group: Gordon Olson. Short and stocky, with ruddy, smiling features and a generally easygoing attitude, he had been selected less for his considerable knowledge of the sport than for his ability to form unusually close relationships with his players. Like every baseball coach, Gordy was part instructor, part taskmaster, part cheerleader, part father. But it was his capacity for deep, familial-type bonds that equipped him to draw the best performance out of any given player. Performance was critical, Casey knew. But more impressive to her had been her uncle's declaration that Gordon's motivation was simply to know, and care for, the men under his leadership.

Beside Gordon sat Herb Madsen, the franchise's newly acquired trainer. Recently released from his contract with one of the "winningest" teams in baseball after personality conflicts with its temperamental star player, Herb was the best of the best in his area of expertise. Uncle Edward had been ecstatic—and surprised—when Madsen accepted his offer to join the Bachelors.

On Herb's left was manager "Dutchie" Larson, apparently ignoring the entire group while cleaning his nails with the blade of his pocketknife—a habit Casey found nothing short of revolting. Knowing that her presence was already an irritant to the group, however, she averted her eyes and refrained from commenting.

Meanwhile, Don Shelton continued to stare at her as if she were some kind of exotic animal. Taking a deep breath, Casey decided to meet his challenge head-on.

"I'm the owner, if that's what you mean. I'm not crazy about the word 'boss.'"

"Neither am I," Shelton bit out.

Casey met his gaze. "Then don't use it," she said evenly.

The man's eyes widened a fraction, and for once he remained speechless. Around the table, the other three exchanged nervous looks. Casey felt the tension mount. For a moment the realization gave her a tiny bit of pleasure. *Good. Let them be uncomfortable. They're certainly not making this any easier for me.*

Then she felt the soft prick of her conscience. *Don't fall into that trap, Casey. Take the higher road.*

At first she ignored the gentle nudging. For once, she had the upper hand, and she wasn't about to let it go that easily.

Then her thoughts returned to the desperate prayer she'd uttered that morning during her time with God: *"Lord, please be with me this morning. Give me wisdom…and help me to say and do the right thing."*

Fighting the urge to shake off the memory, Casey swallowed

her pride and smiled at the men. "I assure you, gentlemen, I am not here to usurp your authority...or to interfere with your coaching. My goal is the same as yours: to make the Bend Bachelors the best team they can possibly be. To that end, I will have opinions and make suggestions from time to time. Whatever it takes to make our team shine, that's my highest priority...as I know it is yours."

Immediately Gordon grinned at Casey, and the moment of tension was magically broken. His response made her smile even wider in return. After years of struggling with a hot temper and short fuse, Casey was trying hard these days to listen to that little voice inside her head. Whether it was God or her conscience—or both—the guidance it gave her was always sound. She was only sorry she hadn't listened more often.

"Yes, well, that's why we're all here," Dutchie broke in. "So enough chitchat. Let's get down to business." Thinking better of his words, he stopped for a moment and gave her a quick, businesslike nod. "Of course you're welcome, Casey, even though I can't say we're happy about the circumstances that brought you." Sadness gripped Casey's heart as she nodded, acknowledging the reference to her loss. "Edward was a good man. But he had a vision for this team, and we're here to make that vision come true. To start out with, I wanted to talk about some of the hot prospects we'll be seeing this week. Some of the guys have already arrived. Ochoco and Houston came in last night. Gibby—Mike Gibson—will be here tomorrow." He cast Casey a somewhat patronizing look. "He's the hot young kid from Northridge."

Casey bit her lip to keep from lashing out. "I know." She had been intimately involved in the decision-making process when her uncle had agonized over whether to invite the undisciplined, but incredibly talented, young pitcher to camp.

Her look of frustration was lost on Larson. "And, of course,

Boyd is already here. He's been working out for a couple of weeks now. What has the staff been having him do, Don?"

The pitching coach gave an exaggerated, throat-clearing noise, as if to make sure he had the attention of everyone in the room. "He's been running like a horse every morning. Has been all winter." He threw a side look at Casey. "Running—any kind of leg work—is critical for a pitcher. Pitching isn't just in the arm."

Casey swallowed hard. "I'm aware of that," she said carefully.

Shelton looked surprised at her answer but went on without comment. "Right now we're focusing on conditioning. We're trying to get his arm in shape…slowly. He'll be increasing speed a little bit every day. Once the rest of the guys get here, the club can start running some group drills.…"

As the man rattled on, Casey seethed. *The nerve of these guys! Acting like I don't know anything about the game. They know I used to play softball for UCLA. They know I've been a sportscaster. We talked about this at our last meeting.*

The first—and only—time Casey had met with the coaches was shortly after the reading of her uncle's will. At the time, their less-than-enthusiastic response to her leadership had been the least of Casey's worries. Her grief had consumed all her emotional energy. Her uncle was gone, and there was nothing she could do about it. Four months later, although the pain was still raw, Casey was finally beginning to find comfort in the things she *could* control, and she was trying to find hope in the future.

Oh, I hope *Boyd makes it onto the Phoenix roster.…* Her coaches were bad enough. The last thing she needed now was an antagonistic pitcher.

"…the Stars really want him," Shelton was saying. "But that rotator cuff injury was bad. He's much improved physically, but I'm not sure if he can make a full recovery. He's pretty confident, but I'm afraid his expectations may be a little unrealistic.

Either way, he's got to prove himself. Even if he proves us all wrong, I doubt the Stars will want to start him out in the bigs this year. He's going to have to start out in the minors, I'm sure of it. Although I'm not certain how far down they'll send him."

Despite her personal opinion of the man, Casey could not help but feel a twinge of compassion as she remembered the hurt and anger on Boyd's face when she said he might play for her team.

"He really thinks he's got a shot at the Stars," she interjected. The four men looked at her in surprise, as if they'd forgotten she was in the room. "Someone should tell him he isn't going to make it."

Dutchie shook his head, and a well-oiled lock of gray hair fell out of place. "Too early for that. That's the point of spring training: players get to show us what they've got. Right now, we don't have reason to believe that Boyd's got much of anything. But he could surprise us."

"True," Casey acknowledged. "What about Gibson? Think Phoenix will snatch him up?"

Gordon shook his head. "They'll definitely want an option, but they won't play him right away. He's pretty green. He's still got to prove himself."

Dutchie looked at Madsen. "What about it, Herb? Who have you got your eye on?"

In response, the trainer described several players who seemed especially promising.

"How about John Cortez?" Casey suggested after listening patiently for several minutes. As a sportscaster, she had followed the athletic career of the college all-star. "He's a great hitter and an *incredible* shortstop."

Once again the men stared at her, as if dumbfounded by the fact that she was actually attempting to participate in their discussion.

"Cortez? Huh." Herb scratched his chin. "I think I remember a Cortez, but I'm not sure. We have so many guys coming to camp. Are you certain he was invited?"

It was finally more than Casey could bear. She slapped her palms down on the table dramatically, causing the men's travel mugs to slosh coffee onto the white-topped table.

"What do you mean, *you're not sure?* You've got the list, Herb, and you have a mind like a steel trap! You know exactly who you want to see." She felt her cheeks grow hot with anger, and she struggled to keep her voice down.

"Okay, so he's on the list." Madsen shrugged. "We'll see what he can do. But he was one of your uncle's favorites. We're not really all that interested in him."

"Why not?"

"We're just not." Madsen looked uncomfortable.

"Herb?"

"Actually—" he hedged, "we've pretty much decided on Larry Hatch and Hector Barrientos."

Casey looked at her trainer in disbelief. "What do you mean, you've pretty much decided? We haven't even seen them yet. Besides, I told you over the phone I wanted to have input."

The man looked angry. "It's too bad your uncle hired us, since you obviously don't trust our judgment."

"Herb! That's not it at all, and you know it. This isn't about me getting my way. It's about me having a *voice*. I would have liked to share my opinions about Hatch—and Cortez and Barrientos—before you made up your minds. Larry's a fine player, but he's wild and undisciplined. I don't think he's got the maturity yet to handle himself at our level. Send him to single-A."

Herb sighed. "I'd rather not get into this."

"Why not?"

"I...I just don't want to argue with you."

"How come?" Casey realized she was starting to sound like a ten-year-old throwing a tantrum, but she felt unable to let the issue pass.

The man opened his mouth as if to speak, then snapped it shut.

"Go on," Casey urged. "I can take it."

"I just don't see how it can help. I don't believe you know as much about this game as you think you do," Herb admitted. "I can't tell you not to come to our meetings, obviously. But discussing any particular issue just seems like a lose-lose situation."

Casey looked at the other men. "Is that what you all think?" she asked, trying hard to keep the hurt out of her voice. Dutchie studied her carefully, as if deep in thought. Gordy stared at his thick red hands. Only Don Shelton met her gaze, and there was triumph in his eyes. No one spoke.

"Look," she said carefully. "I realize that you don't know me. Just as you're watching the players to see how they perform, you're watching me. I *know* you are. The difference is, you're giving these players a fair shot. I can't prove myself, can't show you what *I've* got, if you won't even include me in your discussions. What I said before is true: I'm not out to undermine your authority. But I *am* going to have opinions."

"And if we disagree?" Shelton challenged.

"Then we'll argue."

The men seemed to consider this.

"Who will win?" Herb asked. "The one with the power, or the one who's right?"

Casey managed to crack a small grin. "You sound awful sure that they won't be one and the same."

Herb could not be swayed. "What if I'm the one who's right?"

"I guess we'll cross that bridge when we come to it," Casey said.

No one spoke for several minutes. Finally Casey broke the silence. "You know, this doesn't have to be a crisis. We don't *have* to agree on this or any other issue. And I don't have to be right. The important thing for the ball club is simply that we have open discussions. We'll all have different opinions. Let's pool them and see what comes of it."

Although no one stepped forward to embrace her suggestions, Casey felt encouraged by the fact that, at least for the moment, the men seemed to be thoughtfully considering her words.

Then Don said, "What about Hatch?"

Casey sighed. "Go ahead and pencil him in. I'm open to seeing how he does...but I'd like to keep Cortez in mind as a backup." The men looked relieved. She raised one hand to the tight muscles at the back of her neck and rubbed absently. "Look, we've got a lot of ground to cover. We've got the players to discuss, plus a few matters regarding business operations. I'd also like to let you in on a few promotional ideas I have in mind for the first half of the season. Why don't we take a break and walk off some of this tension? We'll meet back here in fifteen minutes and pick up where we left off."

Her last suggestion was received enthusiastically by the men, who seemed eager to leave the unpleasant conflict behind them. As the group rose and scattered, Casey dug into her purse for spare change, then headed down the hallway in search of a coffee machine and some badly needed caffeine.

She'd barely gone thirty feet down the tiled corridor when she heard a voice calling after her. "Hey! Wait up! I want to talk to you."

Casey spun on her heel and found herself face to face with a very grim-looking Tucker Boyd.

3

The main idea is to win.

JOHN MCGRAW, NEW YORK GIANTS MANAGER

Casey smoothed a sweaty palm against her right trouser leg, the soft linen cool and comforting beneath her trembling hand.

"Boyd. What's on your mind?" She managed to keep her expression and voice noncommittal. There was no way she was going to let this guy draw her into another argument. Not here. Not now.

As she stared at the man in front of her, Casey couldn't help but notice that he looked a little too neat in his freshly laundered practice pants and new, bleached-white shirt bearing the word *Stars*. She was accustomed to seeing him in the throes of a game, drenched with perspiration and covered with diamond dust, where he had led his former team to victory so many times in the previous five seasons. She noted the number on his new Stars jersey: 99. Teams didn't usually assign such high numbers to training camp invitees they anticipated keeping. Snapshot memories of Boyd flickered through her mind, and she felt a fleeting touch of sadness as she realized that the man who had brought so much to the sport might have seen his last major league game.

"I—uh, was just thinking. What I said before was—" Tucker broke off uncomfortably and ran a strong hand through his thick dark hair. "That is, I shouldn't have snapped like that."

Not if you want to keep playing baseball for the Stars' farm team, Casey thought cynically.

"Apology accepted," she said politely. "Now if you'll excuse me—?" She unconsciously rattled the change in her left hand and glanced around. "Maybe you could point me toward a—"

"Coffee machine?" Boyd supplied helpfully.

"How'd you guess?"

"Are you kidding? At this hour? I'm about to go into caffeine withdrawal myself." Then Tucker grinned, the same goofy, lop-sided grin Casey had seen him offer to the children who were his biggest fans—not counting, of course, the young female groupies—and suddenly, absurdly, she noticed that his eyes crinkled up just a bit as silent laughter danced in his eyes.

"Come on, I'll spring for it," he offered gamely. "Seems like I promised to buy if you'd leave me to pitch in peace."

Casey shifted her weight from one foot to the other. "Hmm—I did leave, didn't I? But you're not pitching."

"Nope. I'm not feeling too peaceful either," Boyd admitted. "Come on." He reached out, touched her elbow ever-so-slightly with gentle fingers, and began to lead her down the wide empty hallway.

Casey fell into step beside him, matching him pace for pace with her long athlete's legs, as naturally as if she had been doing so for years.

"Black, please," Casey directed when they had reached their destination. While he made his selections from the vending machine, she leaned against one white wall and breathed deeply, enjoying the scent of perspiration and excitement—a scent that filled all major sports facilities.

After spending $1.35 to get two forty-five-cent vending-machine coffees, Tucker walked toward Casey triumphantly, bearing two Styrofoam cups that sloshed with a nasty-looking brew. Leading her out a side door, Tucker directed Casey to the practice field and offered her a seat on the brand-new, bright red bleachers.

She sat as she was directed, but looked at him uncomfortably. "I only have a few minutes, Boyd. Is this something we should talk about when we have more time?"

"No, no." He gave a nervous laugh and sat down beside her. "Actually, the quicker the better. Kind of like ripping off a Band-Aid." When she didn't smile, he became more serious. "Okay, okay. I just wanted to say that I was out of line earlier. I shouldn't have said what I did. It's just that…well, I'm a little sensitive when it comes to the game. Something about what you said hit all my hot buttons. I got mad, and I took it out on you. I'm sorry."

Casey scratched a pattern into her cup with one thumbnail. "Are you really?"

Boyd leaned back against the lacquered boards and gave her an odd look. "You don't believe me?"

She shrugged and continued to fidget with her cup. "Maybe. I suppose you think you're sorry. But why? Because you were rude to me, or because you've realized how it may affect your possible future with my team?"

Boyd drew in a quick, sharp breath, his expression cooling slightly. "I've already told you: I have no intention of playing for your team."

"I know, I know," Casey said impatiently. "You're going to be a Phoenix Star. But what if you're not ready?" She swallowed a gulp of the lukewarm brew in her cup.

"I'm ready," he said grimly.

"What if your arm isn't—"

"I'm ready," he repeated.

Casey sighed. "What if the Stars' front office doesn't believe that?"

"Then I guess I'll—"

"What? Play for their farm team? Take the only opportunity you have left to show them what you've got?"

Boyd stared at his feet for several minutes. "All right," he allowed finally. "I suppose there's a chance that I could end up with your team for a game or two. But that's not why I'm apologizing." He looked up, and when his eyes met hers, she could not turn away. "I'm apologizing because I think I insulted a very spirited, very strong woman. And I suspect she's someone I don't want to offend." He looked at her curiously. "Are you always this suspicious of people's motives? Don't you think you're being a little paranoid?"

She squirmed. "It's been a long time since anyone's apologized to me without having an ulterior motive."

"I'm not just anybody," Boyd said with conviction. He reached out a rough hand and placed it firmly on hers, bringing warmth to her chilled fingers. "I say what I mean, and I always tell the truth."

Looking into his rich hazel eyes, Casey found herself starting to believe him. "All right, then," she challenged. "Tell me how you'd feel about working for a woman."

Boyd arched his eyebrows in surprise. For a moment, he stared across the field, as if considering how to answer. "I assume you mean you," he said, stalling. Casey did not even bother to nod. "I—can't say that I would be thrilled," he admitted.

"Why is that?"

"It's not that I think women are less capable. It's just that—well, for one thing, you're young—"

"So are you." Casey couldn't remember how young. She tried to recall the man's stats: *2.05 earned run average, 93-mile-per-hour left-handed pitch, named to the American League All-Star*

Team 3 times, 29 years old, a former college star and minor league pro, 6'2", muscular and tan... Oops, those weren't stats. Nervously, she averted her eyes and took another long sip of coffee.

"—there aren't many women who have spent a lot of time on the baseball field," he finished with patience.

"That's ridiculous!" Casey said hotly. "That's not a valid criterion for ownership. Very few team owners have ever even stepped on a field. But, if you must know, I've spent plenty of time in the ballpark. I was a catcher during college, all four seasons. On scholarship." That sounded weak, even to her own ears.

"Softball," Boyd supplied.

Casey bristled. "Well, for goodness sake! You can't hold it against me that I didn't play on the *men's* baseball team! Besides, I was a sportscaster for over two years, and I grew up playing and loving baseball. The kind of experience you're talking about is required of the coaching staff, not the owner."

Tucker held his arms up in a gesture of surrender. "Look, I said I was sorry. You asked me an honest question; I gave you an honest answer. I'm not interested in fighting."

Suddenly, Casey realized that she was leaning forward in her bleacher seat and was practically nose-to-nose with Boyd as she argued animatedly. Forcing herself to sit back, she added calmly, "And I said that I accept your apology. I'm sorry. I don't want to fight, either." She took a deep breath and willed herself to settle down. "I suppose you think I'm a little oversensitive. It's just that—"

"You don't owe me an explanation," Tucker said gently.

"I know." For the first time, Casey smiled. "It's just that I've received a lot of verbal abuse the past couple of years, and it really gets to me sometimes." She rolled her eyes in exasperation. "I just don't know what gets into people. I mean...all right, so I was a female sportscaster, and now a team owner. But that doesn't give people the right to be nasty, no matter how much they may dislike seeing a woman in those roles." Casey took one last swallow of her almost-chewable coffee, then crumpled the thick white cup in her hand. "I've got to get back to my staff meeting. We have a lot to cov—" She broke off at the expression on Boyd's face. "What?"

"That's it!" He stared at her in horror. "'A female sportscaster.' You're *that girl!* I *knew* I'd seen you someplace before…"

Uh-oh.

"Oh, boy." Casey sighed. "I was wondering if you'd remember that. Look, I made a mistake. I was green, I was trying to help…I got in over my head, and I said the wrong thing."

"I believe your exact words were: 'It's only a game.'" Tucker stared at her as if she had grown a second head, his earlier apology completely forgotten. As a look of disapproval fell over his features, Casey felt her stomach muscles knotting up once again.

"You *know* what I meant." Suddenly, she wanted to cry. *I can't believe this is happening. Just when we were finally starting to make peace.…* "I was just trying to point out that your ability as a player isn't determined by one game."

Boyd looked unconvinced. "That's not what you said at all."

Casey's eyes narrowed, and her melancholy began to fade into anger. "Look, I thought you said you weren't here to pick a fight?"

"I'm not. But there is one thing you should know—" He stood and began to pace nervously. "Whether I play for the Stars or your team…or any other, this isn't just a game to me. I play to win, or I don't play at all. If you want nice players on your team, go recruit yourself some Boy Scouts. If you want professionals, you're going to have to act like a professional yourself."

Casey felt each word like a blow.

"You can't be worried about whose feelings are going to get hurt," he continued mercilessly. "This is a cutthroat, blood-thirsty, dog-eat-dog game. Especially at your level. In the majors, everybody wants their team to win. In the minors, every player has one goal in mind: getting himself to the show. Forget team spirit. You've got a bunch of guys out there who are looking out for their own futures." Boyd stood abruptly and turned, as if to walk away. Then he spun to face Casey once more.

"And if I were you," he warned, "I wouldn't get in their way."

That night, Tucker stared out the window of his four-star hotel room. Below, the sixteenth tee of the resort's famous golf course stretched out before him, bathed softly in moonlight. But he looked upon it with unseeing eyes. Only one image filled his mind: the sad face of Casey Foster as he called her to task for a mistake she'd made over two years before.

But what did she expect? *"Just a game."* Just a game? That's like telling a brain surgeon: "Don't worry about it. Everyone makes mistakes. It's just a life."

A tiny voice inside his head seemed to whisper that it wasn't the same thing at all, but Tucker skillfully ignored the gentle prodding. He knew what he thought. He knew what mattered. He had been kicked down to the minors because he'd gotten weak. He'd suffered an injury and some bad luck along the way, but he was on his way back up. This was a time for hard work, determination, and single-minded focus. He did not have room in his philosophy for "It's only a game."

And he didn't have the energy to invest in a team owner who looked like she might burst into tears at his admittedly overzealous outburst.

Tucker dropped the fistful of fabric from his hand and let the curtain fall.

Beautiful and spirited or not, he didn't have the time to waste on Casey Foster.

All right everybody, line up alphabetically according to your height.
CASEY STENGEL, HALL OF FAME MANAGER

TUESDAY, MARCH 11—PHOENIX, ARIZONA

Crack!

Casey watched in dismay as yet another batter connected with one of "Big Time" Boyd's once-famous fastballs. Groans echoed throughout the stands, and Casey realized the horrible truth: It looked like "Big Time" wouldn't be pitching in the majors for a long time. If ever.

On the field, Boyd watched, slack-jawed, as the ball sailed high up into the morning sky. Despite the fairly cool spring temperatures and arid Phoenix climate, his body was drenched in sweat.

"What's the *matter* with him?" Al Clements, the Stars' manager, asked his pitching coach, Martin Hall. Several feet away, Casey shivered in her olive-colored Henley shirt and khaki shorts. She inched a little closer, trying to catch what the men were saying. "Is it his shoulder?"

Hall looked puzzled. "I don't think so," he said. "He seems to have recovered completely."

"Then what's the problem?"

Hall dragged one hand down his face in a dramatic gesture, pulling his features long and tight. "I don't know," he said in exasperation. "The guy's in prime condition. About a third of the time he throws 'em harder and faster than anyone I've seen. The rest of the time his sizzle turns to fizzle. He's got the rhythm, the drive. He's following through. His form is flawless. But it's like—" The pitching coach thought for a moment. "Like he has no heart. He's *stiff*. Not physically, but *inside*. It's like he's...bored, or something."

"Well, can't you get him excited, for crying out loud?" the bald-headed Clements bellowed.

Hall shrugged. "I don't think it's something he can control. He *wants* to be here. Wants it bad. But his head is the only part of him with passion anymore. Sometimes that's enough. Sometimes it's not. He's just—"

"Inconsistent." Clements spat the adjective out like a swear word.

"Yeah," Hall agreed. "Inconsistent."

"Well, that's just great." The manager sat for a moment, deep in thought. "All right then," he finally sighed. "Cut him loose."

The pitching coach looked startled. "You mean send him clear down to A-ball?"

"Nah. No point. Looks like he's lost his nerve. Besides, we've got Lopez, Chapman, Witherow, and Campadore to start the season. And we'll start Gibby with the Bachelors and pull him up as soon as he's ready."

Casey's heart sank. Although the Stars had invited Boyd to training camp, they weren't obligated to sign him. They didn't even need to recruit him for one of their farm teams.

"If you say so—" Hall was scribbling furiously on his clip-board.

"Excuse me?" Casey slid onto the bench beside Clements and flashed her best on-camera smile, all the while thinking, *I can't believe I'm sticking my neck out for that yahoo.* For reasons she could neither identify nor explain, she could not shake the mental image of a dejected-looking Tucker Boyd facing the prospect of life without professional baseball. "Mind if I join you, gentlemen?"

"Of course not! Always room for a lady," Clements beamed.

"That's very kind of you." Casey swallowed hard, choking back the nausea she felt whenever she had to schmooze. Carefully, deliberately, she moved to a seat on the bleachers one row below the coaches. During her stint as a reporter, she'd learned to set high boundaries—both physical and emotional—with the sports figures she met. In this case, the action was likely unnecessary. She'd known Al Clements, a friend of her uncle's, for years. Still, one could never be too careful. She needed to be friendly, but she wasn't about to give either man reason to think she was flirting with him.

"Guess Boyd's having a bad day," she said offhandedly.

"And it ain't about to get any better," Hall mumbled.

"I guess that's to be expected from a guy who pitches ninety-three miles per hour," Casey said in a casual tone. "No one can keep up that kind of performance forever. I wonder how long this dry spell is going to last." She'd been watching the field and the object of their conversation, but now turned to look directly at the two men. "I'd sure like a chance to find out. What do you guys say? What are the chances of you letting me have Boyd—at least for a few weeks—to help stir up local excitement for my team? Once he's warmed up again, we'll let you have him back."

Clements and Hall looked at each other.

"Come on," Casey wheedled. "You know you've got enough pitchers to start the season. Besides, you've already promised me Gibby, and it will be good for the kid to work with Tucker. Boyd has *way* more experience under his belt. Maybe some of it will rub off on Gibson." *And maybe some of Gibby's good fortune will rub off on him,* she prayed silently.

"We-eell…" Clements pretended to consider her request. "I don't suppose we need him right away." He bestowed a benevolent smile upon her. "All right, he's yours! Just don't say I never gave you anything. Ha, ha!"

Casey pasted a look of amusement on her face, while Hall shook his head in disbelief. "You're too much, Clem," she said with as much conviction as she could muster.

Way, way *too much.*

TUESDAY, MARCH 18—PHOENIX, ARIZONA

Feeling more like a den mother than the owner of a professional baseball club, Casey surveyed the sea of young faces surrounding her. She had met several of them before and had even been involved in their selection: Niemeyer, Ferraro, Steinkamp, Fretheim, Harris, Heath, Kosterman, McInnes, Lainez, DeRoos, Esposito. Others had been chosen exclusively by her coaches: Gibson, Hatch, Barrientos, Vazquez, Cage, Ochoco, Holmes, Ojeda, Murphy, Walker, Daly, Gainer, Houston. Some of the men wore expressions of curiosity as they tried to determine what Casey's level of involvement would be. Other faces betrayed a sense of frustration at being sent down to the minor leagues—and the domain of a woman.

After a long-winded speech about the virtues of building a winning team, Dutchie Larson turned the meeting over to Casey.

She wanted to wipe her damp palms against her spruce-colored, polar-fleece pullover but knew the gesture might betray her nervousness, so she tucked them casually in the pockets of her shorts.

"Thanks for your time, gentlemen," Casey began. "I'll keep my comments brief. We all have a lot of work to do." She began to circle the room, making eye contact as she spoke.

"As you know, the Stars have made their selections—as have the Bachelors. It is my pleasure to welcome each of you, and to congratulate you on being selected as the first lineup to represent this new minor league expansion team." She grinned. "Since this is our introductory meeting, I guess you could say we're having our very first Bachelor party!"

A few of the players responded with nervous laughs. Others just stared.

Casey swallowed hard. *Whew. Tough room.* "Sorry." She cleared her throat and smiled halfheartedly. "Just trying to break the ice. Look, I know that there's a lot of tension here. This is—" At that moment, the door opened and a sullen-looking Tucker Boyd entered the meeting room. Casey acknowledged his late entrance with a nod as he went to stand beside his fresh-faced counterparts. "This is a fantastic opportunity for everyone here. I'm sure that many—if not all—of you are hoping to be moved up to the majors during the season." As if of their own volition, Casey's eyes strayed over to Boyd. "We all know such opportunities are rare. The Stars have already chosen their team. But believe me, if you do your job well, it won't go unnoticed. However—" Here, she gave the pitcher a pointed stare. "It's important to remember that regardless of your personal goals, we *are* a team, first and foremost.

"I'm not trying to force anything on you. I don't expect an 'instant family' connection here. But you won't have to go looking for opportunities to get to know each other well. There will be plenty. The horror stories you've heard about the minor leagues are all true: you'll be traveling constantly—by *bus,* living out of motel rooms, and—well, let's face it, you've all had individual discussions with us regarding your salaries. Take one good, last look at Star City. 'Cause the memory is going to have to last you all year. There's nothing glamorous about minor

45

league ball." Here, Casey stopped and grinned. "But there *is* something *wonderful* about it. Something pure and unspoiled. Something exciting and mysterious. Anything can happen—and it probably will!" She paused for a moment, knowing she'd need to frame her next comments carefully.

"For some of you, this season represents just the beginning of your career. For others, as we all know, it will be the end. That's the nature of baseball. So we've got one season, one summer and fall together, as a team. One opportunity to bring baseball back to a town that recently lost it. If you've ever felt a love for the game—not for winning or succeeding, but for simply *playing* with every last fiber of your being—then this is the time to live out that passion. *This* is the time to live out the fantasy that millions of other men only get to dream about."

"Yeah. Sharing a locker room with a woman!" cracked one young voice.

At that, the entire room erupted in nervous laughter.

Casey scanned the crowd and immediately singled out her heckler: nineteen-year-old Larry Hatch, the shortstop her coaches had favored over John Cortez. She groaned inwardly, realizing that her assessment of his maturity level may have been even more on target than she had feared. While the other players quickly regained their composure, boisterous pitcher Mike Gibson continued to laugh heartily at Hatch's side, and Tucker Boyd looked on disapprovingly.

"Sorry, Hatch," she deflected the harassment easily. "I'm not that kind of girl." She flashed the boy a quick grin that said, *I'm in charge here.*

As she continued, most of the men appeared visibly relieved that there would not be a confrontation. "Seriously, though. Larry has raised a good point. Some of you may be worried about exactly that issue. Believe me, I have no interest in coming into the locker room. If I had to, I could. My responsibilities as a sports reporter took me into that situation repeatedly, and I managed to conduct my interviews in a professional manner." She refrained from mentioning the catcalls, innuendoes, and outright insults she'd often received.

"However, we'll have plenty of other spaces where we can meet as a group. As a team owner, there will be no reason for me to enter the locker rooms, unless there's some kind of emergency. So, as long as Gibby can keep from slipping on the soap and giving himself a concussion," she joked, "I think you'll all be safe. Are there any other concerns?"

"Just one." Casey's heart sank at the sound of Boyd's voice. From his position at the right of room, he called out: "I haven't heard you say anything about our goals for the year. You mentioned becoming one big family, but I didn't hear anything about winning. As long as I'm here, I'm here to win."

"You better believe it!"

"Tell her, Boyd!"

"You said it bro'!" All around him, young players whistled and slapped high fives.

Casey looked at him directly as she said, "I believe Dutchie covered all that before you arrived."

Tucker ignored the commotion around him and focused on Casey. "I'm not asking about Dutchie's position. I'm asking about yours."

"My goal is to make this team the best it can be."

"So you want to win?"

Casey shrugged and once again tucked her hands into the generous pockets of the shorts she wore, hand-me-downs from her brother that she had cinched up tight around her waist. "If that's what being the best entails, then I suppose I can look forward to a season of victories."

Boyd looked exasperated. "What *else* would be involved in becoming the best?"

Casey threw him her best Mona Lisa smile. "I guess we'll just have to wait and see."

As the men continued to hoot and cheer, Casey realized the meeting was beginning to crumble all around her.

"All right, all right.... hey, guys. *Guys!*" After several minutes, they returned to some semblance of order, but she knew she needed to wrap things up quickly.

"Over the next two weeks we'll be reviewing fundamentals, getting in shape, and gearing up for the season. You each have your individual schedules, and you are responsible for following them. Let us know if you need any help with travel arrangements, okay? Now, come here. Gather 'round in a circle. Just for a minute," she urged.

Once the men had formed a rather lopsided oval, she explained. "I want to end this first meeting with a word of prayer." Without stopping to weigh their reactions, Casey bowed her head and prayed: "Lord, thanks for these men. Nothing is an accident or a coincidence when it comes to your plan—least of all the selection of a group such as this. We look forward to the year ahead and thank you for the opportunities, blessings, and times of personal growth to come. Please be with us as we travel, and bring us all safely to Bend. In Jesus' name we pray, Amen."

Around the room, several men mumbled an embarrassed "Amen."

"Thanks, guys! By the way, you're all invited to a team prayer meeting next Monday morning, and every Monday morning till the end of the season. I figure we might as well start out on the right foot. All right, now, get out of here. We'll see you tomorrow morning, nine o'clock!" With that, Casey flashed the group a friendly smile and turned to leave the room.

As she spun around, she caught a glimpse of Boyd out of the corner of one eye. He was watching her, and for once his eyes were not filled with a gleam of irritation, but with an expression of bemused curiosity—or perhaps it was grudging admiration.

He lifted one hand in a tenuous wave.

And to her surprise, Casey's heart began to sing.

Poets are like baseball pitchers. Both have their moments.
The intervals are the tough things.

ROBERT FROST

THURSDAY, APRIL 3—BEND, OREGON

Casey leaned back in the office chair, her feet propped up on her battered metal desk, and blew away a wild lock of hair that had fallen into her face.

"Yeah, everybody made it, Clem," she said, tapping one tennis shoe against the other. "Uh-huh. Practice started on Monday." She listened to the prattle of words from the Stars' manager. "You bet. We'll keep you posted. You think you'll want Gibby when? Six weeks? I don't know.... What about Boyd?" she said hopefully. Just because she'd stuck her neck out for the guy didn't mean she wanted him moping around her ballpark all summer. "Not for a while, huh? Sure. Oh, yeah. You bet. That's great for us." *Just great...*

For the next fifteen minutes, she listened patiently as Al Clements shared his insights about several players chosen by the Stars. Then he began to question her about her own team.

"What about Cortez?" he finally asked. "I thought you wanted him." Inside, Casey seethed. *I did....*

"Well, there's still time yet," she said lightly. "We'll see what happens."

"What do you mean, there's still time?" Clements grumbled. "If you want the kid, go get him."

"We'd have to let someone else go," Casey explained unnecessarily.

"Who'd you have in mind?"

Casey bit her lip. For all his overbearing attitude, Clements really had been a close friend of her uncle's, and she knew she could count on his full support. But "running to Clem" wasn't likely to win her any friends on the coaching staff. This was a problem she was going to have to solve on her own.

She pushed up the sleeves of her soft gray terry sweatshirt. "Not sure, yet. That's part of the problem. We've got a good, strong roster. I'd hate to cut anybody."

In the distance, Casey heard the crack of a bat. She wiggled her feet nervously, itching for the chance to get outside and watch.

"Hey, the guys are starting up. I think I need to get out there, Clem. Thanks for talking. I'll keep you posted. Say hi to Bev for me." With that, she was off and running.

Out on the field, Casey found that Gibby, Ochoco, and Houston were throwing for batting practice. Off to the side, a frustrated Don Shelton was glumly watching an out-of-sync Tucker Boyd.

"This is the worst he's looked yet!" Casey whispered in dismay as another pitch spun wildly out of control.

"Yup," Shelton agreed.

"Hey, Boyd!" she called out. "You're rotating too soon. Wait until your landing foot hits—"

The pitcher paused, one foot in midair, and stared daggers at her. It was clear that there was nothing the man wanted *less* than her opinion, but she could see the problem clearly and wasn't about to remain silent.

"You're timing's off," she explained. "You've got to feel the

51

energy moving *up* your body," she urged as Tucker lowered his foot to the ground. "At foot strike, let the energy load your legs, hips, torso—before your throwing arm snaps the release. Come here, I'll show you...." She moved to his side, laying soft, gentle fingers on the rough, sun-dried skin of Tucker's muscular arm.

"You've got to be kidding!" Boyd sprang back as if she had stung him, and a war of emotions seemed to play itself out on his face: displeasure at being the focus of her unwanted advice, and something subtler that Casey could not define.

She forced herself to tear her eyes away from his pained expression. Tucker's emotions were none of her concern. His pitching was. "No, I'm serious," she insisted, reaching for the ball. "Your leg and hip are rotating horizontally out of sequence. There's a way you can—"

"Sorry," he interrupted, annoyance apparently winning the battle of emotions. "I don't mean to be rude," he said coolly, "but I'm really not comfortable taking instruction from an ex-coed softball player who thinks this is 'just a game.'" He turned to Shelton with a look of irritation on his face.

Casey struggled to control her rising anger. "I was just going to have you do a 'reach-out-and-touch-someone' drill," she explained calmly. The exercise had been a favorite of her uncle's, one that he'd taught her as a teenager to help her "feel" the action he was trying to teach.

Shelton nodded with grudging approval. "Good idea. Do it with her, Boyd."

"But—"

"Do it!"

Stiffly, but obediently, Tucker moved back into position. Casey stepped forward and placed herself in front of him. "Okay, Boyd. Show me what you're doing. Let me see where your foot lands." She grabbed the ball out of his hand and watched as he reluctantly wound up and followed through with an imaginary pitch.

Placing herself about four feet in front of his maximum stride, she raised her hand in the air, as if preparing to receive a high five. "All right, now. Go through another delivery, but keep your eyes on my hand and try to slap it." Boyd looked at her as if she was crazy, but did as he was told.

"Good." Casey backed up about six inches. "Now do it again." The second time, Boyd had to stretch out farther in order to reach her fingers. "One more time." She continued the drill until Boyd could no longer reach her hand.

"Come here, Don," she called to the pitching coach. "Look at the length of his stride."

"Huh," was Shelton's only comment.

"Almost a foot longer. And check out his rotation. You see? The feet deliver the torso with no rotation of the upper body until his landing foot touches down—*then* the torso rotates while the upper body and throwing arm keep going forward."

"Keep going," Shelton directed. Casey and Boyd repeated the actions several times until the coach was satisfied. Then she stepped back and let Tucker try a few more pitches. The difference was like night and day. Even Boyd looked pleased at the vast improvement.

"Woooo!" Casey threw her arms in the air and hooted enthusiastically. "Perfect! You've got it!" Tucker glared at her as several other players abandoned their drills and came over to watch. Casey smiled encouragingly as he stepped back a bit from her and his coach. "You've got it down cold, you know. You're just a little tense. Don't worry so much about what you know in your head. Try to let yourself feel it in your heart."

Boyd stared at her incredulously. "My heart? Is that a technical term? I don't feel this in my heart."

Casey gave him a knowing look. "Maybe that's your problem," she said quietly.

By this time, a small crowd had gathered as the men surveyed the spectacle of their young owner stepping in to direct the former superstar.

"Lookin' good, Boyd," Ferraro told him.

"It's no big deal—" Tucker told him, looking thoroughly embarrassed by the attention Casey's coaching had drawn.

"No, really, nice form. You've got a good stretch going there," one of the other rookies insisted.

"Good coaching, Foster," Niemeyer praised her.

Boyd gave them a look of disgust.

"Must be beginner's luck," Hatch suggested.

"Or all that prayin' she does!" Gibby called out with a laugh. "Maybe God told her how to pitch!"

Casey just chuckled and threw the guys a grin. Despite the fact that thus far only Niemeyer and Gordy had come to her prayer meetings, she hadn't given up on the rest of the guys yet. "I don't think God has any favorite ball clubs. But he *does* work in mysterious ways. Guess you'll just have to come on Monday if you want the inside scoop!" The laughter died in her throat, however, when she saw the expression on Boyd's face as he turned away.

Although she'd truly wanted to help him, she realized that she had also managed to embarrass him in front of his peers. And despite the fact that she was finally gaining the respect of many of his teammates, the knowledge of Boyd's displeasure somehow stole the joy that might have come with that small victory.

6

It's not whether you win or lose, it's how you play the game.
GRANTLAND RICE, SPORTSWRITER

THURSDAY, APRIL 17

Casey yawned and stretched from her position on the grass as she watched the sun sink low in the sky, feeling a weariness unlike any she had experienced since her own days of playing college ball. At her elbow, just below the sleeve of her white T-shirt, a mosquito made an aggressive attack on her skin. Casey disposed of him with one quick slap of her Bachelors' cap and sighed.

The week had been a long one. Her days were so packed with activities, she was barely taking the time to eat properly—a sure sign that she was under higher-than-normal stress. Her irregular schedule had also made it difficult to stick to her early-morning workouts. So far this week, she'd only snuck in two, and she could feel the results in her well-toned body.

Kicking her long, slender legs out in front of her, she let her eyes rove over what had once been a beautifully landscaped ballpark, but now resembled nothing so much as an empty battlefield. After nearly three weeks of intensive instruction, workouts, practice, and drills, huge dirt potholes had been dug into the infield and loose tufts of grass and dirt lay scattered artlessly across the rough-looking diamond.

Casey surveyed the scene approvingly, though. It was exactly as it should be. The men were working hard—in spite of the fact that only a couple of them had a real chance of making it to the majors. Boyd, should he miraculously hit his stride again, and Gibby, the "can't miss" rookie. None of them had the highest-paying job on the planet, but most seemed grateful just for the opportunity to be playing ball. Aside from a few of the cockier young boys, the players had thrown themselves wholeheartedly into their training. Her only regret was that she could not be out there with them.

Spying a loose ball that had lodged itself under a nearby stretch of bleachers, Casey impulsively stood and walked over to retrieve it. Beneath her fingertips, the leather was soft and warm from the afternoon sun. She raised it to her nostrils and breathed in the pungent scent of leather and dirt and human sweat.

She glanced around. At six-thirty, the stadium was long abandoned. Practice had ended at one-thirty, and even the most dedicated players had straggled away a few hours ago—after taking extra batting and fielding practice—while Casey remained in her office, juggling finances and schedules and plotting promotional events to draw in local crowds for the Bachelors' quickly approaching opening season.

Turning the smooth leather object in her hands, she walked across the diamond, stepped up to the pitcher's mound, and laid two fingers across two seams for a fastball. Just for a moment, she was twelve years old again.

As a little girl, pitcher had been her favorite position on the ball field. Yet as she grew older, it became clear that her greatest talent lay elsewhere, and in college she'd earned a reputation as the finest catcher in UCLA's history. Yet, occasionally, she couldn't help but wonder, wistfully, what it would have been like to strike out her most dreaded opponents....

She turned her cap around, pointing the bill toward the back. Then, setting her body in position as Uncle Edward had instructed her, she slowly raised her arms over her head and freed her pivot foot for placement. Keeping her right foot beneath her lift knee, Casey raised her left leg to maximum height while bringing both arms down in front of and close to her chest. Pausing briefly, she found her center of gravity, creating a straight line from the ball of her pivot foot through her torso to her head. From this balanced and tall position, she let herself fall forward. As the ball of her landing foot touched ground, she felt the power of her action flow up through her legs, body, and arms, then on to the baseball as she prepared to release it.

"Hey, Foster!" a voice rang out. "You're rotating too soon. Wait until your landing foot hits!"

As she let loose a crazy, out-of-control pitch, Casey spun around, mortified that she had been caught in her own world of fantasy baseball.

Clearly amused by her reaction, Tucker Boyd stepped onto the field and explained in a tone of exaggerated patience: "Your timing's off." He patted her arm gently, as if speaking to a small child. "You've got to feel the energy moving *up* your body," he said. "Remember: legs, hips, torso, arms. Energy, *energy!* Come here, I'll show you."

By this time, Casey was laughing hard, her embarrassment forgotten. She pulled off her cap, allowing her auburn, chin-length hair to fly, wild and untamed, about her face.

"Okay, okay. I deserve that!"

"Seriously, though," Tucker's playful expression altered almost imperceptibly as he reached out to touch her arm. "Let me show you." Without waiting for permission, he stepped in close behind her and laid his hand over hers on the baseball. "Go ahead and wind up." As the faintest flicker of excitement trembled within her, Casey obeyed, while Tucker followed each fluid movement with his own well-muscled body.

As she completed her follow-through, he drew back and said in a quiet, ragged voice, "Nope. Nothing wrong with the way you move." Then, as Casey looked up at him wordlessly, he mumbled under his breath, "Although it might not be a bad idea to try that again."

Casey tore her gaze away from Tucker's face and stared at her hands, which were beginning to tremble beneath his. What was she thinking? What were they *doing*? She didn't know this man. She didn't even *like* this man! Or did she? The strange little feeling in the pit of her stomach alarmed her. But whether she liked him or not didn't matter. He clearly hated her. *It's hormones, Casey. He's not the first ballplayer to make a pass at you. Just walk away, like you always do.*

"No, thanks." She cleared her throat and pointedly stepped aside, pulling her arms away with a twinge of regret. Tucker let Casey's physical withdrawal go unchallenged, although by the expression on his face, she could tell that it had not gone unnoticed. "I learned my lesson two weeks ago." Wiping her sweaty hands against her loose-fitting khaki shorts, she tried to adopt her most professional tone. "I owe you an apology, Boyd. I shouldn't have jumped in on your practice like that, without warning. I know I have to earn the players' trust—*especially* yours, after that whole Seattle fiasco." She turned and began making her way back toward the stands.

"I have to admit, I wasn't exactly thrilled when you did that," he acknowledged, falling into step beside her. "I've been thinking about what you said, though, and you were exactly right."

After weeks of emotional sparring and posturing, Casey felt

awkward at his sudden bare honesty. "Which part was I right about? Your rotation being off or you not feeling baseball in your heart anymore?" She laughed uneasily. "You'll have to narrow it down for me. I'm right about so *many* things."

"Very funny." Tucker's lips twitched in amusement, a habit Casey found strangely endearing. Oddly enough, despite his appreciation for her attempt at humor, he did not pursue the subject further. Instead, he gently tugged her down beside him on the bleachers, then stretched out his arms behind his head in a casual angle of repose that was almost regal.

After a moment of awkward silence, Casey touched his sleeve. "I'm sorry. You were being serious. I shouldn't have made a joke."

Tucker patted her hand. "Don't be sorry. I just—" He stared out over the grandstand, as if looking for some sign that would give him the words to speak. "I'm not sure how to do this, but I'd like to finish something that I started weeks ago." He paused again. This time, Casey waited patiently until he was ready to continue. "On the day we met at training camp, I began to apologize for being rude to you," he said. "You thought I had ulterior motives."

Casey smiled at the memory. "You thought I was paranoid."

He shook his head. "No. You were right. Although I didn't realize it at the time."

"What do you mean?"

"That day, when you lit into me for acting patronizing toward you on the field, I watched you walk away, and I thought: 'Now that's a woman with spunk.' I told myself I had no business talking to you like that, and then I went after you to make things right." As he spoke, he began to play absently with Casey's fingers, which still rested on his arm. Although she knew she should not allow him to continue with such an overly familiar gesture, she could not bring herself to pull her hand away.

Tucker seemed unaware of the effect his simple action had on her emotional state. "Then, when I realized who you were, something inside me just snapped," he went on. "I realized that I was feeling very drawn to a woman who seemed to completely misunderstand baseball—the thing that most clearly represents what I am about."

Swallowing hard, Casey ignored the comment about Tucker being "drawn to" her and focused on the part she thought she could cope with. "The fact that I owned the team didn't help?"

"Are you kidding?" Boyd snorted. "That only made it worse. I could just see you make the official team motto: 'It doesn't matter whether we win or lose.'"

Casey laughed. "Or, how about 'Winning isn't everything'?"

Tucker groaned. "Ugh. Exactly. I don't know what happened after that. I kind of shut down, I think. Something about you just...*irritated* me to no end."

Casey felt a strange feeling of disappointment in the pit of her stomach. "Gee, thanks a lot," she said dryly.

"No...no, that's not what I mean," he told her quickly, half-laughing. "I liked *you* just fine. A little *too* much, maybe." This last comment he made under his breath. "The problem was, I hated what you stood for."

"You're kidding? What was that? Good sportsmanship?" Casey quipped.

"No." He let her teasing pass without comment. "I disliked you because you didn't seem to give the game the respect it deserves. But besides that, in my eyes you stood for something I consider to be truly terrible: the press."

"Oohhhh!" At last, understanding dawned on her. "I get it. You've been raked over the coals during the last couple of seasons."

"Forget the coals. I've been through a full-fledged bonfire," Boyd grumbled. "I haven't been treated fairly by a single reporter. When I was on a winning streak, everybody thought I was the greatest thing since sliced bread. Now they say I'm a no-talent, good-for-nothing waste-of-space."

"What do *you* say you are?" Casey asked softly.

Tucker seemed to consider this. "Do you know," he said thoughtfully, "you're the very first person to ask me that? Everyone else has it figured out already."

She gave him an impish grin. "Maybe I have, too."

"All right, I'll bite. What's your diagnosis, Dr. Foster?"

Casey shook her head. "*Unh*-unh. You have to go first."

"We-ell." Finally, he let her fingers drop. Brushing off the feeling of disappointment, she drew them back into her lap and folded them neatly into a gesture of self-control. "I'm not sure," Boyd answered. "Maybe I've lost my nerve. I still *know* what to do. I'm in the best shape I've ever been in. But...it just doesn't feel right anymore. The flow is all wrong. It's like I've lost—"

"Heart?" Casey supplied.

This time, Boyd did not react in anger. Rather, he seemed slightly amused at her suggestion. "Now, how did I know that was coming?"

"Don't worry," she assured him. "I won't beat a dead horse. I told you what I thought once. That's enough." As if of their own volition, her fingers circled around his once more in a quick squeeze of reassurance. "But I want you to know that I *am* here if you want to talk about it."

"Why? Because you're the owner of my team?" Tucker searched her eyes, as if preparing to weigh her response.

"Because I care," she said simply.

Boyd nodded slowly. "I believe you really do." He grimaced. "That's what has made this so hard."

"What do you mean?"

Dark eyebrows pinched together in an expression of extreme frustration. "This whole time I've been angry with you,

61

you've been nothing but kind—"

"Uh, well…" Casey started to protest.

"All right," he admitted with a laugh. "Maybe not *kind*, exactly. But you've been up-front and honorable in all your dealings with me. Even when you've been angry, you've been gracious. I felt worse than ever when I found out you're a Christian."

This struck Casey as odd. "Why is that?"

"You might not know it, after the way I've been acting these past few weeks, but I became a Christian way back in college, after going to several meetings of a sports-related fellowship group. I got real excited about it for a while, but…well, to tell you the truth, once I got out of school and started playing ball, my spiritual commitment sort of got put on the back burner. I'm not a real big churchgoer these days, but I do believe in God, and I don't think he would like the way I've responded to you as another Christian."

Casey let that sink in for a moment. Then she said, gently, "You know, you're not the only one at fault here. I've had a chip on my shoulder ever since Seattle. I'll admit that I blew it."

Feeling restless, she stood and began to pace. "Believe it or not, Tucker, baseball isn't 'just a game' to me, either. When I was growing up, I used to spend every waking moment playing or dreaming about baseball. The kids on my block would run around the diamond day and night, chasing after pop flies and sliding into home until our clothes were torn and our hands and knees were bleeding." As she spoke, Tucker watched her with a deep intensity.

"Our moms thought we were nuts," Casey continued passionately. "And maybe we were! But to me, nothing compared to standing out in that dirt field, feeling the sun warm my back, and sharing laughter and once-in-a-lifetime moments with the friends I loved most. For years, before they switched me to catcher in high school, I dreamed of achieving what I believed to be the height of beauty: pitching a perfect game."

As she spoke, Casey saw walls of mistrust fall away from Tucker's eyes as he identified with her words. "For twenty years, this sport has been one of my greatest passions," she told him. "But the reason has nothing to do with the number of games I've won. It has to do with community—the sense of connecting with the other players, of sharing an incredible life experience. Baseball isn't a one-on-one competition. Could you imagine playing by yourself? Throwing to no one? Hitting the ball out of the park with nobody there to see it?"

Her eyes implored him to understand. "*That's* what I mean when I say that winning isn't everything. It's part of the fun, part of the joy, the miracle of the entire experience. But without the people, it wouldn't mean a thing. The value lies in the players, the fans, the coaches…the living, breathing fellow participants who share the sport we love.

"That's one of the reasons I chose the career that I did," she confessed. "For years, I'd heard stories about players' egos and inflated salaries ruining different sports. After I started reporting, I witnessed unbelievable conflicts between management and players—not to mention discrimination and sexual harassment. I'm not just talking about baseball. There were problems across the board. But I chose sports reporting because it was something I knew and loved—and I wanted to make a difference. I wanted to contribute. I wanted to be a part of the solution, rather than just complaining about the problem.

"And do you know what I got for my trouble?" she asked, her voice strained with frustration. Boyd shook his head. "I got insulted and harassed for being a woman sports reporter." She looked at him earnestly. "I was so careful, Tucker! I realized that I had to go into the locker rooms to get interviews after the games, but I kept my behavior above reproach. I was always very professional and respectful. I stayed in areas where I knew the guys would be fully clothed. The way they've got things set up these days, it's easy for a player to shower and dress before facing the press in the locker rooms. But still, there were guys who tried to get me booted out.

"There were a few who actually got a kick out of picking on someone they saw as 'weaker.' But for the most part, the guys thought that what they were doing was right. They figured a woman's place is…well, not on the sports field, anyway. In their minds, they were sticking up for men's interests and encouraging me to go back to where I belonged.

"A couple of those guys I knew to be Christians. I needed their support, but they made it really hard. For a long time I struggled with that. I even took a step back from God for a while. But immediately, I felt a void in my life, and I had to draw closer to him again. Eventually, I realized that God wasn't the one who was treating me poorly. It was a handful of guys— not *all* baseball players, not *all* men—just a few players, a few coaches.

"That's when I started seeing the same thing in myself, in reverse. I became bitter toward men and overly defensive when it came to the way I was treated on the job. I expected the worst from people. I'd get angry, and I was often rude—just like I was to you. And it showed in my work. I can't tell you how many times I jumped all over some coach's or manager's offhand comment that I took wrong. Believe me, it didn't help my career any. There's a reason I wasn't getting any promotions," she admitted ruefully.

"But just like those guys who made me so angry, I justified my behavior based on my feelings. It was the dead ends in my career that made me see what was happening. After Uncle Edward's death left me this tremendous responsibility, I decided to leave sportscasting and honor his wish for me to stay involved with the team. I figured that I'd have as much impact here as anywhere. But I'm still battling with feelings of anger and frustration—and how I can respond to those emotions."

She looked at Tucker and hoped he saw the gratitude in her eyes. "So, thank you for apologizing. I respect the fact that you want to treat me well because I'm a child of God. But you know, as Christians, we need to treat each person we meet with equal respect. God wants us to be loving to everyone he brings into our lives, whether they are Christians or not. So I would like us to encourage each other to grow in our relationships with God, and to let those relationships impact our interactions with others."

Throughout her entire speech, Tucker had listened without comment, never once allowing his deep hazel eyes to stray from her face. Now, he reached out one hand and, in an intimate gesture, brushed back a stray lock of hair that had fallen against her cheek. "You make a convincing argument," he said quietly. "And I'd like to say I'm ready for that, but I'm not sure I am. I *do* care about God...but I'm not sure I can forget about winning."

"Oh, Tucker! I'm not asking you to forget about—"

"Shh." One strong, rough finger came to rest against her lips. "We're not going to beat a dead horse, remember? I'll think about what you said," he promised with a weak smile.

"Well, that's all I can ask," Casey admitted, then reluctantly turned away. Despite the fact that she suddenly felt she could spend the entire evening talking with him, she knew she had no excuse for enjoying Tucker Boyd's company any longer.

As if reading her thoughts, he rose beside her and asked, "What are you doing now? Is there any chance I might get to steal you away for an apology dinner?"

Casey struggled to hide her strong feelings of pleasure. "Well, I really should stay and finish some paperwork...." As she stalled, her thoughts raced. Was he asking her out? Did she actually *want* him to ask her out? The funny little stomach flips resumed, settling that last question once and for all. But she was the team owner. Tucker played for her...worked for her. What was company policy on such a thing? Oh, my goodness, she *was* the company....

She glanced down at her rumpled shorts and dirt-covered white T-shirt. "I don't know. I'm not really dressed for—"

Tucker threw up his arms, not accepting her argument. "Don't worry about it," he interjected. "I'm not either." Casey considered his attire: loose-fitting jeans, a stylish madras shirt, and tennis shoes. He looked much more put together than she, but vanity was certainly no reason to refuse his invitation. *The question is, Casey, how badly do you want to go?*

"All right," she said decisively. "Let's go."

"Great!" he said approvingly. Casey laughed as he wrapped his fingers gently around her wrist and pulled her along beside him. "And don't worry about what you're wearing. It's not a big deal. We'll just grab a pizza or something."

For a moment, Casey's heart sank. *Wonderful. So much for this being a date.*

But for some crazy reason, as she allowed herself to be led away, Casey Foster could not stop grinning.

7

With the kind of year I had, I'm ready to try anything.
PAUL HOUSEHOLDER, CINCINNATI REDS OUTFIELDER, ON GETTING
ENGAGED IN THE OFF-SEASON AFTER BATTING .211, 1982

Setting aside her fork, Casey grabbed a crispy tortilla chip from the basket on the table and used it to scoop generous helpings of sour cream and guacamole onto her plateful of sizzling fajitas.

Directly across the table from her, Tucker focused his energy on busily digging into a mouthwatering chicken-and-brown-rice creation, upon which he had slathered the hottest salsa the restaurant had to offer.

"Umṁm!" Casey mumbled happily, unable to articulate more clearly around her mouthful of juicy steak and green peppers.

After giving it considerable thought, the two had decided against Tucker's earlier suggestion, in favor of more health-conscious fare. Despite the fact that Bend offered some of the best pizza she had ever eaten, Casey was thrilled with their ultimate choice: a trendy Mexican restaurant with funky decor and outdoor seating, located at the heart of the town's charming downtown district. As they ate, they watched the tourists strolling by the quaint little shops and restaurants on their way to Drake Park and Bend's popular Mirror Pond.

While gobbling up their mouthwatering fare, Casey and

Tucker made the usual getting-acquainted small talk. They quickly discovered that—as they'd each suspected—they were the exact opposites in many ways.

Tucker, Casey learned, was the intense, unbending perfectionist she had suspected him to be. By the time she had finished her second fajita, he had her laughing over stories about his college days and the hysterical conflicts he'd had with his slobbish roommates. In turn, he was horrified by the fly-by-the-seat-of-your-pants attitude with which she approached life.

Tucker had grown up in the Midwest, where baseball was almost a religion. Casey had developed her love for the game on the West Coast, where it was simply looked upon as a valuable form of entertainment.

Even their tastes in music were different. Casey's favorite songs included older tunes by James Taylor, Carole King, and Joni Mitchell, although she preferred listening to more upbeat pop/rock tunes when working out. Tucker was a true-blue classical music snob.

Yet, despite their differences, the two were surprised to discover that they also shared many similarities. Both were runners—Tucker ran eight miles a day, five days a week, while Casey's commitment varied and her runs were more sporadic. Both were avid sports fans who enjoyed playing games infinitely more than watching them. Both were committed to giving their all to any challenge they tackled. And both agreed that the value they treasured most in a relationship was truth.

Above them the vivid blue sky was streaked with color as the sun headed toward the western horizon. "You've got sunshine over three hundred days a year in this town," her uncle had told her proudly, after scanning through the city's tourist pamphlets two years earlier. Since then, she had heard many of the locals complain that such claims were highly exaggerated, but she was in no mood to dispute them now. There was nothing quite as breathtaking as a summer day in the high mountain desert, and although spring had not yet said her last good-byes, this evening the Central Oregon climate was at its invigorating best.

"Well, I have to admit, I never would have thought it," Casey said, reaching for another warm tortilla.

"What's that?"

"This. Us. Having dinner together like two rational people. I mean…it's laughable." She accidentally demonstrated by half-chortling, half-choking on a forkful of refried beans. "Two years ago, I thought you were the biggest creep I'd ever met."

"And now?" Tucker watched her carefully for a response.

Casey's bright blue eyes widened. She hadn't expected that question. "And now…I don't," she finished lamely.

"Very good. Nice evasive move," he joked.

"Stop it!" Casey threw her napkin across the table at him. "You don't seriously expect me to answer a question like that."

"Don't I?"

By now, she was laughing hard. "Bo-oyd…"

"Come on," he urged. "Humor me."

"We-ell…"

"And make it something nice," he suggested helpfully, handing back her napkin with exaggerated politeness.

"Fishing for compliments, are we?"

"Go on. I'll make it worth your while."

"Hmmm. That sounds promising. Okay, let's see. Something nice…something nice…" She drummed her fingers against the table dramatically. "Gee. Something *nice,* you say…?"

"Ha, ha. Very funny. Keep it up, and you forfeit your turn."

"All right, all right." Casey settled back and laid one hand against her taut stomach muscles as she considered his request.

What did she think about Tucker Boyd? That was a tough question—and one that had been playing over and over in her mind for several weeks.

Before she'd met him again at spring training, she'd been convinced that he was a pompous, self-absorbed egomaniac, whose greatest concern—or perhaps *only* concern—was his performance on the playing field. Any earlier impressions regarding the pitcher's kind behavior toward his young fans was obliterated by the black mark that her own interactions had left on Casey's memory.

Her suspicions had been confirmed the day she'd met him again, out on the field. With his cocky attitude and pro-baseball grin, he'd tried to dismiss her as a groupie, without even considering the possibility that she might have been on the premises for a legitimate reason.

From beneath long, thick lashes, Casey snuck a quick glance at the object of her critique. Looking relaxed and comfortable for the first time since she'd met him, the large man almost—but not quite—managed to fit in with the cheerful vacationers around them. In this environment, with his golden eyes twinkling and the early-evening sun bringing out little hints of red in his thick, dark hair, it was hard to remember her negative first impressions. In fact, it was hard to remember anything at all....

Stop it, Casey, she told herself. *It doesn't matter what the guy looks like. Besides, you're going to embarrass yourself. So, think...*

When had her impression of him begun to change? Perhaps it was that day over coffee, when he had cut straight to the chase and apologized for his earlier behavior. Possibly her opinion was still colored by the opportunities she'd had, as a member of the press, to watch him signing autographs for his fans with the kind of sincere kindness that could never be faked. Or maybe her change of heart had to do with the genuine anguish she'd seen on his face when he'd realized at spring training that his performance truly was slipping. The level of pain he'd demonstrated went much deeper than ego. Clearly, he had been a man facing the very real possibility of a terrible personal loss....

"It's that hard, is it?" Tucker's words were teasing, but his expression was solemn.

"Oh, no!" Casey protested. "I was just remembering."

"Remembering what?"

"My first impressions."

"Ugh. Those can't be good. I was a bit rough on you in Seattle."

"Maybe. But actually, that wasn't the first time I'd seen you up close."

"Really?"

"Mmm-hm. I'd interviewed a couple of your teammates a couple of months before that, when the team came to San Francisco. Couldn't get close to you, though, you big super-star!" She couldn't resist the dig.

He threw up his hands in a gesture of defense. "Don't look at me! It wasn't my decision. If you'd asked me, I'm sure I would have given *you* an interview."

"Oh, really?" she said, with raised eyebrows. "I gather you're a sucker for the ladies."

"No, no. Nothing like that."

Casey just stared at him.

"Okay, okay," he admitted, looking a bit uncomfortable. "Maybe it was *something* like that. But it's not what you think."

"It makes no difference to me," she protested, a little too fiercely. But to her dismay, Casey realized suddenly that she did care—very much, in fact—what Boyd's relationship with other female reporters might have been.

"I'm not a wolf, Casey, if that's what you're thinking."

"No-oo." Even to her own ears, the word sounded unconvincing.

"I won't pretend that I haven't dated quite a few women—"

"Stop!" Casey threw her hand up in the air, as if to silence him. "Tucker, please! This is silly! I never asked…I don't need to know this."

"I know," he assured her. "But I'd like to tell you. Please?"

Grudgingly, she settled back in her seat and folded her arms across her chest.

"Certainly I've had plenty of opportunities to meet women," he continued. "But I am *not* a man on the prowl."

"You sure were quick to invite me to coffee," she said shrewdly. "Twice."

"That's right," Tucker agreed. "And it wasn't a coincidence that you were the first reporter I called upon after that game in Seattle."

"Ohhhhh," she groaned. "Here we go again!"

"Casey!" he laughed. "Sure, you made me mad that day. But you also intrigued me. You had spark. It's the same thing that drew me to you at the ballpark."

"Really?" She wanted so much to believe him….

"Really. If I'd really thought you were a crazed fan after me, I'd have walked away."

"I'm surprised you didn't anyway, after what I said to you…." She recalled with regret the way she'd insulted him when he asked her to leave the field.

"Not a chance."

Casey waited for him to elaborate, but he just grinned. "So what you're saying is that you're… I mean, you wanted to talk with me further because—"

"Because I'm attracted to you?"

The bluntness of his words startled her. She was used to asking hard questions, not receiving them. "Ye-es, I suppose that's what I'm asking."

Tucker reached out and gently folded her hands in his. "Yes, Casey," he said, with just the hint of a smile. "I am very attracted to you. I have been from the very beginning."

Although she'd instinctively known where their conversation was heading, Casey felt shocked to hear the words spoken out loud. She remembered the way he'd singled her out of the crowd in the Seattle locker room. "But you said you wouldn't have given me an interview just because of my looks!"

"Well, maybe that's an exaggeration," he said playfully. Casey couldn't help feeling amused by his honest admission. "I never said I didn't like what I saw of you. I just meant that I also liked what I saw *in* you."

Casey felt a delicious chill run up her spine. "And what was that?" she said breathlessly.

"The same thing I see today: a very passionate woman who cares deeply about the people around her. A woman who knows what she wants and goes after it. A woman who knows that she deserves respect and is willing to fight for it—"

Abruptly, Casey pulled back, unintentionally pulling her hands from the warmth of his grip. "I *wish*," she sighed. She was still kicking herself for having backed down about John Cortez.

Tucker raised one eyebrow. "What? What did I say?"

"Oh, just that part about fighting for respect." For an instant, Casey wished she could draw comfort from the warmth of his hands once more. At the same time, it was a relief to have the tension of the moment broken. "It seems like whenever I try to stick up for myself, I shoot off my mouth and get into trouble. At other times, I just sit back and let myself get walked on."

Boyd nodded knowingly. "Like with Shelton. And Hatch."

Casey looked at him in surprise. "How do you know about that?"

"I've seen them both be pretty rude to you. Shelton can be pushy anyway, but he's probably worse with you. He's just one of those guys who think women have no business in sports."

"Ugh. Not *another* one." Casey rolled her eyes.

"Hey. Be fair. We aren't all like that. There are plenty of men out there who treat women as equals."

"I know, I know," she admitted. "But even *you* had a hard time with me—"

"Not because of your gender," he said, "but because of your experience level. I think it's the same for a lot of other guys."

"Maybe." In her head, she knew it could be true, but her heart had a hard time believing it.

"You know what you need to do?"

"Take a three-month vacation?" she said morosely.

"Very funny. No, you need to stick up for yourself."

"I knew *that* was coming."

The look Tucker gave her was one of understanding. He stood, grabbed the back of his chair, and drew it alongside hers so that they sat close together, but without touching. "Casey, you know what you're doing in this job. You've been proving it since day one. I know it stinks that you have to work so hard at something the rest of us take for granted, but you're doing well. Just keep at it. Never quit."

Casey gazed into the deep hazel pools of his eyes. "Is that what you tell yourself about pitching? 'Never quit'?"

Boyd thought for a moment. "Maybe."

Drawing confidence from his closeness, she asked boldly, "Would you want to keep playing baseball if you knew you could never win again?"

A shadow fell over his eyes. "Sounds like a nightmare to me."

"Okay, let me rephrase that. Let's say you can be assured you'll win games. But you'll lose just as many. No pennants. No awards. No fame."

"No success."

"I didn't say that."

Tucker shook his head. "It's the same thing."

"Is it really?"

Leaning back against his chair, he turned his face away and watched a group of teenagers roll by on in-line skates.

After several long moments, Casey tried again. "Winning really is important to you, isn't it?"

He nodded abruptly. "It really is."

"Do you mind if I ask why?"

"I don't mind. I may even try to explain, but I'm not sure if I can put it into words, exactly."

He considered his words carefully, then began. "I grew up in the Midwest. Both my parents were factory workers. Before he met my mom, my dad played a lot of baseball as a kid. He was an incredible hitter. He could have played professionally, but before he was old enough, both his parents died, and he had to give up baseball and take a factory job in order to feed his younger brothers and sisters.

"It was a loving thing to do, but eventually he grew incredibly bitter. By the time his youngest siblings were grown, he had gotten married and had—" The words seemed to stick in his throat. He had a son of his own. His dream was long gone.

"And so he threw all his energy into teaching his son how to play ball. When it turned out that I had talent, he was thrilled—absolutely beside himself...*way* more excited than I ever was." Tucker had been looking off into the distance, as though gazing into his past. Now he turned to look into Casey's eyes. "Don't get me wrong. I loved to play. But there wasn't any point in playing if I wasn't going to win. That's what my dad wanted from me. That's what made him happy.

"Year after year, it got harder and harder as my dad's expectations grew bigger. I used to think that he wouldn't love me if I didn't do well. Luckily, I guess, I never found out whether that

75

was true or not." The words came out soft and low. "Dad died of lung cancer just six months before the shoulder injury. He always loved to see me win. When he died, I was still winning."

Casey considered this. "Did he die happy?"

Tucker didn't even have to think about it. "No. He didn't. He was never happy with what he had. He was always worried about the things he had never achieved."

"What about *you*? Are you happy now?" Casey asked gently.

Again, the answer came quickly to his lips. "Not even close."

"Why?"

He shrugged. "Because I'm losing. I'm letting everyone down."

"But were you happy when you were winning?"

That question took a little more thought. "No," he said finally. "I can't say that I was."

"Then what have you really lost?"

"Just my dad, I guess."

Casey nodded.

"What?" Tucker caught the silent message. "You mean, what you were saying before about people?"

"People *are* what matters most," she insisted. "I don't think you're upset about your performance as much as you are still grieving over the loss of your dad."

Tucker looked at her thoughtfully. "Perhaps. What about you? Do you have a good relationship with your dad?"

Casey wrinkled her nose in disdain. "I haven't seen my father since I was fourteen years old. He left my mother, my brother, and me when I was three. Aaron was only one.

"Every once in a while Dad would turn up and take us to a ball game or two. He and Uncle Edward both loved baseball. It was about the only thing they had in common. It was Dad's idea, in fact, to name me after Casey Stengel, and the character in the Ernest Thayer poem, "Casey at the Bat." But he never came to see me play ball. As the years went on, we barely saw him. Eventually, he just never came back at all."

"That must have been hard, growing up without a dad," Tucker said softly.

Unconsciously, Casey leaned a fraction closer to him, to the comfort of his compassion. "It was. I missed having a father around to cuddle me and tell me I was loved. Someone who would do all the wonderful, hokey dad stuff, like teaching me how to ride a bike or grilling all my potential boyfriends."

Tucker grinned the knowing grin of a man who knew the drill of being grilled by protective fathers. "So, did your mom do those things instead?"

"For the most part. All except grilling my boyfriends. She was much too sweet to ever be truly threatening. The rest of the time I pretty much relied on my Uncle Edward."

"Tell me about him," Tucker asked, with real interest.

Immediately, Casey warmed to the subject. "Well…Uncle Edward was my father's older brother, but you'd never know it. They were *nothing* alike.

"Dad was very fickle. He reminded me of a butterfly. He'd flit from one thing to the next, and Aaron and I were like a couple of flowers on the mountain path. Uncle Edward was totally solid." Casey's face lit up as she said his name. "He lived hours away, up in Napa Valley. But he came down to visit quite a bit—for a while there, it was every weekend. I think I saw him more than some of my friends saw their own dads."

"He must have loved you very much."

"We were close," Casey agreed. "I think I spent more time with him over the past two years—talking with him over the phone, or running out to the ranch to go over plans for the team—than I had throughout my entire childhood. This team was very important to him. I could have sold it—I suppose there were quite a few people who wanted me to. But I just couldn't let go. Somehow I wanted to…oh, I don't know. Hold on to a bit of him, I guess…even after he was gone."

"What happened to your brother?"

"Oh, Aaron and I are very close! It's hard to be this far away from him, but we talk all the time on the phone. We both lived in San Francisco for the past few years, only a mile or so away from one another, and he's still there. Until a couple of months ago, he ran the business office of a major software development company…he's a whiz at numbers and a great manager. Uncle Edward left him the vineyard, so he's up to his ears in wine these days, down in Napa Valley. Mom's still in L.A. She remarried a couple of years ago. Jim's a real nice man. He treats Aaron and me well…" Casey's voice trailed off.

The two sat in companionable silence as just a hint of darkness began to fall and the steady flow of foot traffic past the restaurant slowed down to a trickle.

"What are you thinking?" Tucker asked at last.

"Hmmm? Oh, I was just reflecting on what you said earlier. I don't think Uncle Edward would have liked to see me caving in to the other coaches, the way I have. I just don't want to fly off the handle all the time."

"You can do it, Casey. It doesn't have to be a fight. Just talk with the guys. Tell them that you want to treat them with respect, and you expect the same thing in return."

"I don't know.…" Visions of unpleasant conflicts with assorted sports figures gave her reason for caution.

"Well, whatever you decide, I want you to know that I believe in you," Tucker assured her. Despite the gentle breeze that had arisen, Casey felt strangely warmed.

"Well, I certainly have nothing to lose, I suppose. I don't really want to initiate anything at this point. But the next time one of those guys tries to push me—" Her fiery spirit began to rise.

"You don't have to push back," Tucker reminded her. "But you *can* stand firm."

Casey drew a deep breath of refreshing spring air. "You're right. Okay, I'll give it a shot." She eyed him mischievously. "What about you?"

"Huh? What *about* me?"

"Are you ready to take a risk?"

"Like what?" he asked suspiciously.

"Well...Why don't you come to prayer meeting on Monday?" she suggested warmly. "This might be a good time for you to reexamine your relationship with God. He knows all about what you're going through, Tucker. And he really does want to help."

"Prayer meeting, huh?" Surprisingly, the suggestion did not seem to make him uncomfortable, as Casey had feared it might. In fact, the idea actually seemed to appeal to him. "I guess I could be convinced," he said, sounding a bit bewildered yet almost pleased as the words passed across his lips. "I suppose the way things have been going, it couldn't hurt."

They broke it to me gently. The manager came up to me before a game and said they didn't allow visitors in the clubhouse.

BOB UECKER, ON BEING FIRED, 1976

FRIDAY, APRIL 18

For several weeks Casey had anticipated with dread the eventuality of a conflict with either Shelton or Hatch. She had suspected that the moment would arrive sooner, rather than later. What she hadn't prepared for emotionally was the public nature of the challenge she would face.

Her arms piled high with manila folders she'd taken home the night before, Casey headed toward her office the morning after her supper with Tucker. "Uncle Edward never said anything about being chained to his desk," she grumbled to herself as she prepared to tackle what she was finding to be an endless mound of paperwork. It seemed like she was working constantly these days.

As she neared the clubhouse lunchroom, she heard the unmistakable roar of ballplayers laughing uncontrollably.

"Hey, now! Keep it down. *Some* people have to work around here, you know," she called over her shoulder good-naturedly. As she passed the door, a new wave of laughter erupted, and with a terrible sense of dread, she instinctively realized that they were laughing at *her*. But why?

Retracing her steps, she poked her head into the eating area. Resting her stack of papers on one hip, Casey made a quick survey of the men who stood in a semicircle around the lunchroom window: Gibby, Houston, Harris, Ojeda, Daly...and a gleeful-looking Larry Hatch.

"Good morning!" Hatch chortled at her. He threw a disrespectful sidelong glance in the direction of his teammates. "Or should I salute?" Snorting back rude laughter, he contorted his features into a mask of sobriety and snapped his wrist to his forehead, like a soldier at boot camp.

"Salute? Why on earth would you do that?"

Hatch snickered and Gibby giggled as they looked first at one another, then out the window.

Casey set her paperwork down on the nearest table and strained her eyes to see what had captured their attention. As she walked toward the window, a white object over the field caught her eye: bulky and shapeless, it hung heavily from the flagpole, like a misshapen, colorless kite...or a woman's girdle.

"Oh, good grief." Her heart sank. Sure enough, someone had run a voluminous corset partway up the flagpole. It wasn't Casey's; she had no need for such devices. But the gender inference was clear.

This was the last thing she needed. Casey enjoyed a good practical joke as much as the next person. But flying undergarments at half-mast was clearly crossing the line between innocent humor and sexual harassment. She watched in disgust as Gibby clutched his side and laughed uncontrollably. Mike was a good kid. Under normal conditions, he treated Casey with deference and respect. But when under the influence of his immature teammate, Gibby often exercised poor judgment. Hatch's shenanigans were clearly having a negative impact on one of her best pitchers—the pitcher she was supposed to be preparing for major league ball, no less. How would Clem react if Gibson spent his first days with the Stars running around his hotel conducting panty raids?

"All right, that's enough," she said firmly. "This one's just not funny, Larry. I want you to go out there and take it down."

"Oh, come on. Don't be so uptight."

"I mean it," Casey said carefully.

"What's the matter? You don't want to climb the pole yourself? Is your girdle too tight?" At this, the young men laughed so hard, tears came to their eyes.

"Larry, may I speak to you privately?" Casey indicated that he should follow her from the room.

"*Oooo*-oooo," he mouthed in a singsong voice to the other guys. "I think I'm in trouble with *Mo*-om."

Casey gestured for Hatch to step into the hallway, then leaned back into the room. "I want the rest of you out on the field. Now."

"But practice doesn't start for another—"

"I said *now*. Start with fifteen laps."

Looking thoroughly subdued, they moved to comply.

On the way to her office, with Larry in tow, Casey encountered Dutchie and Shelton, heading toward the field.

"How's it goin', Foster?" Dutchie called loudly. He continued down the hallway, not waiting for an answer.

"Gentlemen, I was about to have a word with Larry. Would you mind joining us?"

"Actually, we were just—"

"Please. It will only take a minute." Seeing the intensity of her expression, the men wisely complied.

"What's this all about?" Shelton asked gruffly as soon as Casey had closed the door.

"Awww, it's nothing—" Hatch kicked the toe of one cleat against the other. "We just pulled a little prank, and Casey didn't think it was funny."

"What kind of a prank?"

"You know…the old underwear-up-the-flagpole trick."

The manager and coach exchanged looks of amusement.

"Look," Casey began in exasperation, sitting on the edge of her desk, "I get the joke. My point is that it is tasteless. And it is disrespectful. Yes, I am a woman. But I am also the owner of this team, and I refuse to be the target of crude pranks."

None of the men responded. Of the three, only Dutchie showed the slightest bit of discomfort, and Casey wondered if that was simply because he wanted to get back out on the field.

"Now, I am going to tell you one more time, Larry, I want you to take that thing down."

"All right, all right…I'll do it after practice." The boy shuffled toward the door, rolling his eyes at the other two men. Dutchie and Shelton started to follow.

"Stop right there! We are *not* finished." As anger threatened to consume her, Casey called Tucker's words to mind. *"It doesn't have to be a fight. Just talk with the guys. Tell them that you want to treat them with respect, and you expect the same thing in return.…You don't have to push back. But you can stand firm."*

Oh, but this is too hard, she thought miserably, looking at the three unfriendly faces staring back at her.

And then a favorite Scripture verse of her mother's came to mind: *"God is our refuge and strength, an ever-present help in trouble. Therefore we will not fear."* Casey silently repeated the first lines of Psalm 46 several times before continuing.

"Dutchie, Shelton, Larry…I've attempted to handle this as peaceably as I can, but we really are reaching a state of crisis. I've tried my best to show respect to each member of this team and coaching staff. If you can think of ways for me to do that better, please let me know. Unfortunately, I am not getting that same level of respect in return." She rose from her desk and planted herself in front of them, drawing herself up to her full five foot eight inches.

"This situation is no longer acceptable," she said firmly. "Larry, you need to know that I will not tolerate this type of behavior. You're an incredibly talented young man, but you're also undisciplined and unprofessional. You're late for practices. You stay out late at night drinking and chasing women—and then you come in and brag about it. I can't dictate your morals, but I insist that you stick to your training—for the good of the team. You challenge every rule: from diet to curfew to the number of practice drills required. Worst of all, your attitude is beginning to affect others. I can't have it."

"You're the only one who seems to mind," Hatch accused her.

"I doubt that's the case," Casey said calmly. "But even if you're right, that doesn't change a thing. My opinion is enough."

"Just because you're the owner," Larry grumbled.

"You'll follow the rules because I say so, and I'm the owner. You'll treat me with respect because I'm a person, and every person deserves more than what you've given me." She let that sink in. "You're going to have to toe the line from now on, Larry. If you can't live with our rules, then this isn't the place for you."

"Well, maybe it's *not*," Hatch said sullenly. His eyes drifted from Dutchie to Shelton, as if imploring them to come to his defense.

"Now, now...let's not get all emotional about this—" Shelton began.

"I am not acting emotionally," Casey said, surprising even herself at how reasonable she sounded. "This is a rational decision, and it is final. I need all my players to stick to the rules—and to treat me with respect. No other owner would tolerate anything less, and neither will I. If you've made your choice, Larry, I suggest you go clean out your locker."

"Fine!" His face flushed with anger, Hatch stormed out of Casey's office, slamming the door behind him.

A heavy silence filled the room.

Finally, Dutchie cleared his throat. "You know, if you change your mind, Casey, we can always—"

"I'm not going to change my mind."

"Uh...right." Larson was used to being in charge, and she thought he might challenge her. But thankfully, he raised no further argument.

The pitching coach was not so inclined. "Great." Shelton was almost shaking with rage. "And what are we supposed to do now? Bring in your friend Cortez, I suppose? You've had this planned for weeks, haven't you?" he charged.

"Actually, I haven't. But this *has* been building. Surely you see that."

"Whatever." The coach refused to be drawn in by her reasoning.

"Don, this isn't just an issue between Hatch and me. This is about respect. I need it from the players. I need it from the *coaches*. This antagonism has got to stop."

His gray eyes regarded her with a steely gaze. "Are you threatening to fire me, too?"

Casey stared straight at him. "I'm explaining the way things need to be. If you and I can't come to an agreement, then *something* will need to change. That's not a threat. It's just common sense."

"Sounds like a threat to me." He looked at her with contempt in his eyes.

With every fiber of her being, Casey wanted to shout out: "Then take it as one. Go! Get out of here." Then she heard the gentle whisper in her heart that was gradually becoming her most trusted guide: *Take the high road, Casey.*

She followed Shelton to her office doorway, where he stood, poised to leave.

"If I have any threat to offer, Don," she said gently, "it is simply that we will suffer greatly if you go. You and I may have some personality conflicts, but that doesn't change the fact that you are one of the best coaches in baseball. I respect you tremendously. And I am fully confident that we can work through this conflict as two professionals. I look forward to working with you in the years to come. These months mark the beginning of a wonderful team, and I'm excited about you, the other coaches, and me shaping it...*together.*"

Apparently, Shelton could think of no response to that statement, for without another word, he slipped through the doorway and disappeared. Dutchie moved as if to follow him, but stopped at the door.

"You're doin' good, Casey," he said with feeling and a look of approval. "Your uncle would be proud." And then he was gone.

As she stared at the place where the two men had stood moments before, Casey could not help but smile as she considered Dutchie's words. Somehow, she sensed that he was right.

Uncle Edward would be pleased.

Tucker, too.

And if her hopes were correct, so was God.

⌁ 9 ⌁

After all, I don't think God really cares about baseball.
He's got more important things on his mind.
DAN QUISENBERRY, KANSAS CITY ROYALS PITCHER

MONDAY, APRIL 21

Casey's eyes flew once more to the clock on her office wall. Nine-thirteen. She continued to stare. The hands did not stir.

Across the desk from her, outfielder Steve Niemeyer lounged in a well-worn, cracked-leather chair, gulping down mouthfuls of vending machine coffee, reminding her of the disgusting brew she had shared with Tucker Boyd in Phoenix.

Where is he?

"Looks like Gordon's late this morning," Steve commented unnecessarily.

"Yep." She turned her attention to a stack of papers, pretending to be supremely interested in the tiny lines of type. The silence was slightly awkward. She didn't really know Niemeyer very well yet, but she wasn't in the mood for idle chat. Before her eyes, the characters danced across the page in a steady blur as she struggled to make herself focus.

"Pitching Rotation...Pitching Rotation...Pitching Rotation..." Casey read the heading five times before giving up. She laid the

sheet down in disgust and, leaning back in her chair, peered out the window at the glorious azure sky.

Tucker had said that he would come this morning, hadn't he? She tried to recall his exact words. *"Prayer meeting, huh? I guess I could be convinced."* The statement defied analysis. *Okay, so he didn't specifically say that he was coming* this *morning, but it was sort of implied....*

The sound of a doorknob turning pulled her from her musing. Casey smiled in relief as the door to her office swung inward, revealing...Gordon Olson.

Disappointment crashed over her like a wave, and she fought to hide her emotions, even as she struggled to make sense of them. *Why does it matter so much whether or not Tucker shows up? I'd like* all *of the guys to come. There's nothing so special about him....*

But the words did not ring true. Day by day, she was beginning to realize that there was indeed something very special about Tucker Boyd. She nodded a greeting to Gordon, who was already deep in some training-related discussion with the young rookie.

She was grateful for the opportunity to compose her thoughts. *What is it about Tucker?* she wondered.

During their dinner together, she had managed to worm her way out of answering his point-blank question regarding her thoughts about him. In the days that followed, however, Casey hadn't let herself off the hook that easily.

Who *was* Tucker Boyd?

Well, he wasn't who she had considered him to be at the beginning of spring training. Her eyes came to rest on the assortment of framed athletic awards that decorated her office walls. The man was driven to win, it was true. But she had no business complaining about his competitive spirit; she herself liked to win. And there was no indication that he wanted to win *at all cost*. His compulsion to succeed seemed to have less to do with ego than with an unconscious desire to process unresolved feelings regarding his relationship with his father.

Who was he, then? She didn't know a lot about Tucker, but she *did* know that he was a man committed to hard work, and to helping his teammates reach their potential. Casey had never seen a more dedicated ballplayer. Day after day, he trained as if his very life depended on it, taking breaks only to help others who requested his assistance with their drills.

He was a man with rough edges…and a tender heart. Over the past few weeks she had watched him interacting with others. While he was not overly effusive, Tucker treated everyone with respect—from his head coach to the vendor who filled the ballpark's soda machines. But when it came to Casey, he was sweet and amiable.

A hint of a smile played about Casey's lips as she recalled the various winks, nods, and "speaking glances" he had cast in her direction over the past few days. Unless she was misreading the signs, the man was definitely interested.

And amazingly, she found herself doing the one thing she had sworn she would never do: she was falling for a ballplayer.

The thought alarmed her, but it was not quite the shock she would have expected such a realization to be.

Her aversion to such a relationship had begun four years earlier when, as a twenty-two-year-old communications major in her final semester at UCLA, she learned the complete truth about her father. Through a series of journaling assignments, she'd realized that she still had many questions about her dad and his reasons for leaving the family. Her mother had been reluctant to discuss the issue, but Casey was insistent.

"I know he was kind of flaky," she told her mom. "But what was it that made him want to leave?"

"Oh, Casey." Anna Foster looked miserable under her

daughter's relentless questioning. "He just wanted to go, that's all."

"But why?"

"Honey…" Her mother reached across the oak dining table and stroked Casey's hair. "It wasn't your fault. It wasn't anybody's fault but his. He just got an idea in his head and decided to go."

Casey sat upright in her chair. That was her first clue. "What idea?"

"Oh, Casey! Forget I said anything."

"No! Mom, please!"

At last, Casey had dragged the story out of her mother. Douglas Foster, she explained, had always been passionate about baseball. He had always wanted to pursue it as a career, but had never been disciplined enough to follow through on his dreams. However, by the time Casey was three, he had begun to feel restless in his marriage and decided to move on. The last Casey's mother had heard, he had been unsuccessfully trying to pursue a career in baseball back east. Out of respect for her daughter's love of the sport, Anna had never told her the truth.

Outside Casey's office window, the brilliant spring sun rose higher in the sky. She drummed on her desk with tension-filled fingers. After her father's abandonment and the treatment she had received as a sports reporter, she had sworn that she would never fall for a ballplayer. Especially a major league ballplayer. Tucker seemed different, though.

But was that her head talking, or her heart?

Casey threw down her pen. She was disgusted with herself…mooning after a guy who hadn't even bothered to show up like he'd promised. Maybe Boyd wasn't as different as she'd thought.

"Come on, guys," she said gruffly. "We'd better get started. Practice starts at ten."

She moved around to the front of her gray metal desk and perched on its edge. Gordon drew up an orange plastic, industrial-style chair and positioned it next to Niemeyer.

"Okay, let's talk about prayer requests," she said more cheerfully. After that, all thoughts about a certain superstar pitcher were pushed to the back of her mind as the three of them brought each other up to date regarding a wide variety of individual and team needs.

After nearly fifteen minutes of discussion, Casey opened their prayer session.

"Lord, thank you for this opportunity to meet together on this incredible, *wonderful* day," she began. "You are the God of sunshine, and friends, and even baseball. We are grateful to be here, doing what we love most. We know that you are here with us. And while we don't ask you to favor us above any other ball club, we do ask that you help us perform to the best of our abilities, and to glorify you with our actions and words...."

Over the next ten minutes, the three of them took turns, offering up petitions to God and praising him for his faithfulness and goodness to them. After a time, the period of silence between prayers began to grow longer, and Casey shifted, knowing that Gordon would be about to close.

"Ahem...Father God," a rich-timbered voice broke in. It took every bit of Casey's willpower to keep herself from opening her eyes wide and staring. "I know that it's been awhile since I came to you like this, but a friend told me that you're interested in what I'm going through, so here goes." Tucker took a deep breath and continued. "This is the thing: you know better than anyone, I guess, how I've been pitching. Sometimes I think I've got it down, God. At other times, I just lose control. It's a pretty miserable feeling actually. I just can't help thinking that I'm letting everyone down. I always thought that you made me to be a great pitcher, God. I mean…that's the biggest talent you've given me. If I lose it, I'm not really sure what else you want me to do."

He stopped, seemingly unsure of how to continue. Finally, he settled on: "Please be with the team, God, as we prepare for the season. Help us to do well. Help us to win. Amen."

Casey found his last comments unsettling. After they had talked so much about people being the most important thing, she had thought he understood. But his prayer seemed to be about winning. Then, as quickly as the thought flashed through her mind, the desire to judge him passed. It didn't matter what he was requesting. The important thing was that Tucker was turning to God. Regardless of his motives, he was coming back. And Casey knew God could do incredible things in the hearts and lives of those who sought him.

After Gordon closed in prayer, she opened her eyes slowly and blinked against the room's cool fluorescent lighting.

Tucker stood in the doorway, his hands in his pockets, looking like an embarrassed fourteen-year-old at the front of a class.

"You came!" she said, sliding off the desk and walking toward the door.

"You're glad?" Boyd responded with a grateful smile.

Casey quirked her lips. "Fishing for compliments again, I see."

"Boyd!" An enthusiastic Gordon joined them. "Good to see you."

Niemeyer, too, seemed pleased to see his teammate join their ranks. "Didn't know you were a praying man, but I'm happy to see it."

"I guess I am, too," Tucker admitted slowly, almost as if he had expected to have the opposite reaction.

"Well, the three of you had better pray that you make it to practice on time," Casey told them, laughing. There was nothing she would have loved more than to question Tucker about his thoughts at that moment, but this was neither the time nor the place.

As Gordy and Niemeyer turned and started down the hallway, she laid one hand on Boyd's shoulder. "I really *am* glad you came," she said simply.

"Thank you," was all he said, but his deep hazel eyes spoke volumes.

"If you—" She broke off. How could she say this without sounding like she was asking him out?

"What?"

"I just wanted you to know that if you want to talk about this further, I'm available. To talk, I mean."

His look was one of heartfelt appreciation. "I know." He considered her words. "I think I need some time to absorb all this. But if I have any questions, you'll be the first one I'll turn to."

"Good. And don't worry. I'm not pushing you on this. It's really between you and God," Casey said. "Oh! That reminds me...do you have a Bible?"

Tucker wrinkled his brow. "I've got one, but I'm not sure where it is."

"Here." Casey ran to her desk and pulled out a well-worn leather New Testament. "This'll get you started." She grinned at him. "Now I can be the *second* one you turn to...."

⤙ *10* ⤚

*And I want to thank the tremendous fans. We appreciate every boys'
group, girls' group, poem and song. And keep goin' to see the Mets play.*
CASEY STENGEL, HALL OF FAME MANAGER,
AT HIS HALL OF FAME INDUCTION, 1966

TUESDAY, MAY 6

Hey, guys! Listen up!" Casey checked her watch. Not quite
one-thirty, but that was beside the point. The men had
been training like champions. It wouldn't hurt to let them
off a few minutes early. She waved cheerfully. "Come on over
when you're done!"

Forsaking the worn wooden bleachers in favor of the solid
earth beneath her, Casey dropped to the grass, enjoying the
tickle of the soft blades against her legs as she waited for the
men to finish their practice.

One by one, the players completed their drills, then gathered beside her in a small circle.

"Hey, boss," Tucker joked, tossing her a baseball as he
jogged over to sit on the grass beside his teammates.

Casey caught the ball easily. "Hey, yourself, Big Time," she
said with a grin.

When all of the men had joined the circle, she tossed the ball
high into the air and caught it with a flourish. "Well, gentlemen,
we're almost there!" she said happily. "Our first game is just days

away, and although I'm sure it's written all over my face, I wanted to take a moment to tell you how truly proud I am."

A flush of pleasure crossed many of the young faces, and a few stared at their hands in embarrassment. Several cheered, and then a burst of applause erupted.

Casey strained her voice to be heard above the commotion. "You've worked hard! You've improved tremendously. No owner or manager could ask for more. When May sixteenth rolls around, you'll be great!

"McInnes, Ojeda, Barrientos, Walker..." One by one, she named each player and acknowledged a significant contribution or personal gain he had made during training. "And Boyd..." Despite her effort to keep her voice from betraying emotion, the word rolled off her tongue like an endearment. Casey shot a quick look around the group. Thankfully, no one seemed to have noticed.

"I am thoroughly impressed with your growth," she continued. "As a player. And, even more importantly, as a person." The insights Tucker had shared during their dinner together had been immensely private; she could not mention specifics in front of the group. Yet the difference in his behavior over the past couple weeks was drastic enough that it could not have gone unnoticed.

Several of Boyd's teammates bobbed their heads in agreement with her praise, and a look of pleasure flickered in his eyes.

Casey had to give credit where credit was due, though. Tucker was a caring person to begin with; that part wasn't a change. He was generally happy to help out a teammate—until that assistance meant an interruption in his own practice schedule. That's where the real change was evident—and where his real test began. Patience with others didn't come easily, and his desire for peak personal performance was strong. Yet he *was* reaching out; he was facing the challenge head-on with an effort that warmed Casey's soul.

She brushed an unruly lock of hair away from her forehead and shaded her eyes against the sun. "Our first game is a week from this Friday. If there are any plays that aren't working, any signals you're not sure about, talk with your coaches *now*. If you have any questions regarding your schedule, come see me.

"You've been working like insane *maniacs*—" At this, the men laughed heartily. "And now is the time when it will all start paying off." Unable to remain still any longer, she jumped to her feet and clapped her hands in excitement. Her enthusiasm was catching, and the group followed suit, raising a cheer once more. "This is going to be a *great* season, and I'm proud to be a part of it!"

Wrapping up her pep talk, Casey gave a loud whoop and joined in the revelry, slapping high fives with her outfielders and letting out shrill whistles through two fingers, as Uncle Edward had taught her. The men picked up the battle cry, and Casey found herself being hugged and thumped on the back as if she were a fellow player.

When she found herself face to face with Tucker, Casey stopped in her tracks. Without a word, he stepped close, placed both hands on her arms, and looked at her with eyes that seemed to see into the depths of her soul. With heart pounding, Casey realized that she wanted nothing more than for him to pull her into an embrace, as several of the other players had done. But she knew, as she gazed into the eyes that had the power to hold her spellbound, she didn't want a friendly, brotherly hug from Tucker Boyd. And this was not the time nor the place for any other kind.

Reluctantly, she pulled away, feeling bereft as his hands slipped down her upper arms, to her elbows, then released her gently, as a bird to flight.

Casey absently touched her skin where his hands had been,

then cleared her throat and tried to catch the attention of the team. "Wait, there's one last thing!" she called. After several minutes, she finally had their attention again. "We've been invited to participate in a charity softball game on May fourteenth. I know it's rather short notice, but this is for a great cause—and it could mean a lot to us as a team."

She paused for breath and, as she did so, heard a couple of the players grumbling quietly. *"Next* Wednesday night?" She saw Tucker's brow furrowed.

Feeling nervous about the men's—and particularly Boyd's— response, Casey rushed to explain. "The game is being organized by a local group that works with teens at risk. These folks provide services to kids who are trying to get off the streets: clothes, meals, career counseling...and, occasionally, positive, healthy social activities in which to invest their energy.

"The leaders of this ministry decided a couple of months ago that they wanted to start a softball team. Since then, they've been trying to pull everything together. Some local businesses have donated uniforms, equipment, and silk-screening for the team logo. They've got fifteen kids who are committed already, and several others are interested. Last week they played their first game against the staff of Habitat for Humanity. They're trying to schedule future games with the Red Cross and the YMCA. Right now, they're scrambling, though, trying to find teams to play against. They want to keep their momentum going while they have the kids' interest. I got a letter from their director this week, suggesting that a benefit might be the perfect promotional event for both our teams."

"You're kidding. You want us to play a bunch of kids?" Fretheim said incredulously. "We'll kill 'em."

"Actually, it will primarily be a local exhibition in which we'll play against ourselves. We don't even need to play a full game...maybe five innings," Casey explained. "It will give the locals a chance to get to know you guys while supporting a worthy cause. At the end of our game, we'll let the kids come out on the field and hit a few. They'll be thrilled! Can you imagine, them going home and telling their dads they went up against the famous 'Big Time' Boyd?"

But Tucker looked less than delighted. "Do you realize that next Wednesday is *two days* before opening night? You can't be serious! I can't waste good energy, good pitches, on a preseason charity game!"

Casey's heart sank. She'd half-expected Tucker to protest, but deep inside, she'd hoped he would come through.

"So? I'm not asking you to go out there and pitch to Ken Griffey, Jr. All we have to do is play a few easy innings. They'll promote it on the local news, and we'll get some good media exposure. Best of all, we'll be doing something useful, valuable, with the talents God has given us, helping kids in need."

"What if somebody gets hurt?" Tucker challenged.

Casey rolled her eyes. "You'd have to be an idiot to get hurt at a charity softball game like this. You guys are professionals. I think you can handle it."

By this time, the jubilant mood had been tainted with a hint of unease. But Casey continued, unwilling to step down from her soapbox.

"I know it's not convenient timing. But it takes sacrifice to win, guys. You already know that. You've *all* sacrificed. You've left family and friends back home. Some of you are completely alone here. You've worked hard and long, but you're here because you *love* the game."

As she spoke, Casey's voice rang with passion. "I just want to remind you that there wouldn't *be* any game if it weren't for the fans. We want them to come out on opening night and support us...to give us their money and keep on coming back so we can keep playing. But what are we willing to give in return?"

No one spoke. Not a soul moved.

"I'm not going to *demand* that you participate," she said carefully. "Frankly, I don't want you there if that's not what you want in your heart. All I know is this: If I have to play every position myself, I'm going to be there."

At first, no one even met her eyes. Then finally, after a few moments, Niemeyer stepped forward. "I'll be there, too."

A second later, outfielder Ty Murphy moved to join him. "I want to play."

Next, to Casey's surprise and relief, Mike Gibson came to stand by her side. "Sounds like fun," he said lightly. "What time are they feeding us?" His teammates laughed.

Then, one by one, the players voiced their individual commitments, until Tucker was the only holdout left.

"How about it, Boyd?" Ojeda asked. He stood with hands on hips, as if issuing a challenge.

"Walter, don't," Casey said, knowing no good could come of forcing Tucker's participation. "This isn't a battle. Everyone's entitled to an opinion—although I just voiced mine rather loudly, and rather unfairly." She turned to Tucker and noticed that the curtains of mistrust once more shadowed his eyes. "Even though I really do believe those things, I shouldn't have tried to shame you into thinking the same way. I don't want anyone to feel manipulated. I'm sorry." She turned back to the others and said quietly, but with conviction, "He doesn't have to play. No one *has* to play."

"That's right. We don't have to," Tucker said firmly.

Casey's spirits fell even lower.

"But I will."

Almost immediately, the tension of the moment drained away. And as Tucker stepped toward her, grinning, with arms open wide, Casey waited with rather unsisterly anticipation for the "brotherly" hug that was to come.

Don't pray when it rains if you don't pray when the sun shines.
SATCHEL PAIGE, HALL OF FAME PITCHER, 1974

MONDAY, MAY 12

I cy toes met the warmth of soft flannel sheets as Casey burrowed deep beneath the covers of her queen-sized bed. *Sleep, glorious sleep.* Ever since she'd switched her clock forward in April and the days got longer and longer, her workdays had stretched further and further into the night. Tonight, she hadn't gotten home until eight o'clock. Then, after a quick dinner of chicken-and-vegetable stir-fry and steamed rice, she had thrown herself right back into her paperwork, checking last-minute details until well past midnight.

Casey turned on her side and stretched luxuriously, then sighed. Why couldn't she get comfortable? She raised herself up on her right elbow. With one fist, she punched her pillow into the shape of a small mountain, then threw her head upon it, feeling the satisfactory squish of feathers compressing together beneath her cheek. Yet despite her exhaustion and this comforting bedtime ritual, she still felt restless.

Her thoughts drifted back over the events of the day. Arrangements for the charity exhibition game had been finalized, and everything was coming together for the team's opening day. John Cortez had flown in to replace Hatch, and the rest of the men were performing at peak level.

Except for Boyd.

Still the best player they had—when he was hitting his stride—Tucker continued to pitch inconsistently, alternately amazing and horrifying his teammates with record-breaking fastballs that could not be counted upon to remain within the strike zone.

And still the most intriguing man around, he continued to confuse Casey as he pulled closer emotionally, then withdrew, as if he could not make up his mind how intimate he wanted to be. She never knew what to expect. One morning, he might come in to practice early, pop his head into her office, and surprise her with coffee and bagels. The next, he might spend every moment out on the field—almost as if he was avoiding her.

Briefly, Casey had considered confronting him about his behavior. Yet she did not know what to demand of him, for she herself could not figure out exactly what she wanted.

The intensity of her reactions to the man proved only that there was a strong physical attraction. And if what he had told her that night at dinner was true, Casey had no reason to fear that the attraction was not mutual. But where did that leave them? Chemistry alone was nothing to build a relationship on.

Lying there in the darkness, Casey desperately tried to find rational reasons for opening her life to the man who had inexplicably begun to steal her heart.

She was convinced that beneath his intensity and walls of defense, Tucker Boyd was a man who wanted desperately to do the right thing...a man who was willing to face his weaknesses and shortcomings, no matter how uncomfortable they might make him feel. He was a hardworking man, yet one who could care—and hurt—deeply, when the opportunity presented itself. And although he had let his daily relationship with God lapse, he did seem interested in changing that.

For over an hour, Casey wrestled with her bedclothes and her dilemma, but despite these gymnastics, by the time she had finally started to drop off to sleep, she had come to one very sad conclusion: Attraction notwithstanding, she could not pursue a relationship with a man who did not love God as much as she did. A belief in God was *something*, but not enough.

The flirting had to stop. Her daydreaming about this man had to end.

Casey Foster could not date Tucker Boyd, and that was all there was to it.

With that decision made, she rolled over one last time and began to drop off, just as the telephone rang.

With a great kick of frustration, Tucker managed to untangle himself from the cotton sheets that had entwined themselves about his legs. *Stupid sheets. They've all come untucked again. No wonder I can't sleep....*

But it wasn't the sheets that kept him from much-needed slumber, and he knew it. It had been like this all week. Normally, there wasn't anything that could keep him from getting eight to nine hours of sleep each night during the baseball season. He refused all social obligations in order to focus his energy where it belonged. And there was no subject, other than baseball, that he could not willingly dismiss from his consciousness.

Except for Casey Foster.

Crazy, spirited Casey.

Visions of her laughing sapphire eyes sprang to mind, and his thoughts turned automatically to the day they had first met.

From across the room, he had seen her. She was impossible

to miss. Like a rose among thorns, she had stood out among the usual crowd of middle-aged male reporters. With her tousled hair and fresh-faced complexion, she barely looked old enough to be out of high school, much less college. Yet the look of grim determination on her face told him that she wasn't about to watch from the sidelines. He couldn't wait to hear what she had to say, and had to force himself to sound casual when he acknowledged her.

That she had asked him a tough question hadn't surprised him somehow. But his reaction to her assessment of his performance had come as quite a shock. Tucker Boyd had been accused of poor pitching before. Every guy has an off night now and then. But when the words came out of her mouth, the humiliation was almost more than he could bear.

Now, two years later, her opinion of him had begun to matter more to Tucker than any other human being's ever had—except for his father's.

He reached out with one hand and touched the leather-covered book on his bedside stand.

Casey really wanted him to get his relationship right with God. He could tell. On more than one occasion, she had casually asked if he had given any further thought to their conversation...or if he had, as she put it, "read anything interesting lately." The thought made him chuckle.

Her interest was both touching and frightening. Never before had anyone cared so much about the state of his soul— or gotten so close to the real person inside. Tucker's focus had always been on performance. He hadn't taken the time to get to know the people who might have cared for him the most.

Even his involvement with Athletes in Action during his college years had been triggered primarily by social motivation. He liked the guys on his baseball team who went to the club, and he'd attended with them in order to strengthen his ties with the team. Yet his subsequent decision to become a Christian had been genuine; he wanted to make a commitment to serving the God these athletes knew. However, once he graduated and began his career in professional baseball, his focus had shifted. And somehow he had never gotten back to making his spiritual life a priority, although he never stopped believing in God and the truth of Christianity.

Giving up on sleep at last, he sat up in bed and reached for the book he had glanced through several times over the past few weeks. Perhaps there was something within its pages that would help him....

As he flipped through the beginning of the well-worn New Testament, a highlighted section leaped out at him, and he opened the book to that page, feeling curious about the passage that had been important enough to Casey for her to have marked it with the fluorescent yellow ink.

Matthew 25 was the reference, and after reading the first few sentences, he gathered that it was a story about several men whose master had entrusted them with several pieces of silver, or "talents," before leaving on a journey.

"To one he gave five talents," the story read, "to another, two, and to another, one, each according to his own ability."

The verses went on to explain what each man had done with his talents in his master's absence.

"Immediately the one who had received the five talents went and traded with them, and gained five more talents. In the same manner the one who had received the two talents gained two more. But he who received the one talent went away and dug in the ground, and hid his master's money."

When their master returned, Tucker learned, he came to settle accounts with the men.

The first servant came to the master and said, "Master, you entrusted five talents to me; see, I have gained five more talents." The second man's explanation was the same. To each, their master replied. "Well done, good and faithful slave; you were faithful with a few things, I will put you in charge of many things, enter into the joy of your master."

But the third man, who had been a poor steward of what was given him, received only his master's wrath.

Tucker laid the Bible open before him on the comforter. This was what Casey had been trying to say about the charity game. God wanted them to be good stewards of the talents he had given them. As a feeling of excitement grew within him, he read the passage again. And again.

Then, for the first time in his life, Tucker Boyd experienced the miraculous sensation of knowing that God had just spoken to him through his Word. He heard no voice in his head. There was nothing mystical about the moment. And yet, as surely as he knew that he had been born to play ball, he knew that God had meant for him to read these words at this moment.

Tucker had always known that Casey was different. Finally, he was starting to understand why. And he wanted to know more.

It struck Tucker then that he was at that moment embarking upon a wonderful new journey of discovery.

He wanted to know the truth.

He wanted to know God.

And if God would let him, he wanted Casey beside him all the way.

There was little time to process this revelation, however. For just as the thought had formed in his head, the phone began to ring.

Wondering, absurdly, if it might be Casey, Tucker reached eagerly for the cordless phone. He raised it to his ear, then—after listening for a moment—spoke somberly into the receiver.

"I'll be right there."

Casey rushed through the hallway, her sandals slapping against the slick linoleum as she tried to remember the directions Dutchie had given her over the phone.

After a couple of wrong turns, she finally found the wing and the waiting room she was looking for. Several of the team members and coaches had already arrived and had commandeered two long couches along the left side of the room. Although Casey was fond of her players, even she was surprised by how many had rushed to the hospital to be near their beloved coach. In a small cluster of chairs on the right, a dignified-looking, middle-aged woman sat with another couple who had their arms around her shoulders in a gesture of comfort.

Gordy's wife, Casey thought. Her instinct was to go to her, but the distraught woman was obviously being consoled by family members, and Casey hesitated to interrupt.

She picked an open spot on the couch and sat beside Gibby.

"How is he doing?" she asked.

"Not too good," Mike told her, sounding as if he might cry. "Nora said one minute he said he was feeling nauseous, like he had a real bad case of heartburn; the next minute, he was lying flat out on the ground. She called 911 and the paramedics got him here right away. They say that's a good thing," he said, trying to sound hopeful. "One of the doctors told us that most of the deaths that result from heart attacks happen because a person doesn't recognize the symptoms and waits too long to get to the hospital."

"Well, it's not like he could ignore the last symptoms *he* had," said McInnes.

"No, but—" Gibby started to protest, then realized there really wasn't any point. "I guess you're right."

Casey looked up as a haggard-looking Tucker rushed into the room. His eyes flickered over the scene, then came to rest on Casey. Remembering her earlier resolve, she quickly turned away, but not before registering Tucker's look of stark compassion...and something else she did not recognize.

Just as Tucker joined their small circle, a distinguished-looking man with gray hair and a well-trimmed silver mustache came into the waiting room. After determining that the entire group was waiting to hear about his patient, the doctor brought them up to date on the coach's progress.

"We believe Gordon is stable for now," he announced, "although we are watching him very closely. He's got some major blockage, and he passed a large blood clot through one vein. Now if you'll excuse me, I need to speak with Mrs. Olson." With that, he walked across the room and began to talk with Gordy's wife in low tones.

Casey let out the breath of air she'd been holding. "Thank God." The offhand comment triggered a deeper thought. "Actually, we really *should* thank God."

"He's not out of the woods yet," a grim-looking Herb Madsen reminded her.

"No," she admitted. "But he's still here, with us. That's something."

"We should pray for him to get better," Niemeyer suggested, and a couple of players nodded in agreement.

"What good will that do?" scoffed Eddie Cage, a blond-haired, young relief pitcher. "God's not going to listen to us. If he's going to listen to anybody, it's Casey—or maybe Gordy's wife. I don't know about the rest of you, but I haven't prayed in years. I can't believe that God would want to hear from me now, just because I want something from him."

"Yeah," McInnes agreed. "Besides, he never listened to any of my prayers, anyway."

The complete absence of hope in these statements broke Casey's heart. "Why would you think that?"

The man shrugged. "Because he never answered any of 'em."

Casey clenched her hands in frustration. It made her ache inside to hear McInnes offer that as an excuse. There were plenty of examples in her life of seemingly unanswered prayers. But she had known and loved God long enough to trust that he was there, working in every circumstance. His fingerprints were all over her life.

"How did you want God to answer?" she asked.

That stumped the ballplayer for a minute. "Well...I don't know. I guess I just wanted him to be there—to give me what I needed, or show me what I was supposed to do."

Cage nodded in agreement. "It's hard to trust him when you can't even see him."

Casey tried to think of what she could say that would help these men. "Well, I can't address what's happened in the past. That's between you and God. But I do know that he *was* there before, and he's here now. He *does* want to hear from you. He just wants you to trust him with your heart."

"Do you think it will help, Casey?" asked Eddie Cage. "If we pray, will Gordy get better?"

She wrapped her bare arms across her chest and rubbed them with the palms of her hands. "Maybe. Maybe not."

"Then what's the point?"

Casey considered her words carefully. "I don't pray just for good things, Eddie. And I don't pray because I think I can change God's mind. I pray because I can't *not* pray. I can't imagine going through something like this and not having him to support me. When I pray, I'm not wondering whether or not God is going to help me. It's just such a relief to take something that isn't mine to control anyway, and to give it up to God, saying: 'Here it is, Lord. Do your will. I trust you.' I want to do that with Gordon."

"What do you mean, 'Lord, do your will'? What if he wants to let Gordy die?"

At Eddie's last word, a chill of fear ran up Casey's spine. "Well, if that's God's choice, I can't really question it, can I?" she said, trying to ignore the feeling. "I can be sorry about it and wish it weren't so, but I can't change something that's part of God's plan. The Bible says there is a time for everything...a time even for death. If it's Gordon's time, I can't question that. All I can do is say to God: 'Lord, this is my friend. It is my desire that he get well, and I trust that you can heal him. But if you choose not to, I'll believe that you know what you're doing. I'll trust that you will bring something good out of this situation. And I'll draw my comfort from you.'"

McInnes shook his head. "I don't know if I can do that."

Tucker moved to stand beside him and placed a hand on the younger man's shoulder. "I don't know if I can, either," he said with a tremble in his voice. His eyes searched Casey's. "But I want to try...Casey?"

Without hesitating, she stepped to his side and laid her fingers within the comfort of his warm hand. Following her example, the rest of the group moved closer together, forming one big circle.

"Do you really think God can bring good out of this, Casey?" Gibby asked before they began, a hint of longing in his voice.

Casey looked around at the small cluster of men, shoulder-to-shoulder, as they prepared to enter the presence of God.

"He already has, Gibby. He already has."

∼ *12* ∼

There's sunshine, fresh air, and the team's behind us. Let's play two.

ERNIE BANKS, FORMER CHICAGO CUBS INFIELDER,
AT HIS HALL OF FAME INDUCTION, 1977

WEDNESDAY, MAY 14

Casey glared at the ridiculous-looking woman staring back at her from the bathroom mirror. In her college softball pants and oversized Bachelors jersey, she looked almost a decade younger than her twenty-six years. "Oh, brother!" she mumbled. How on earth was she going to make any kind of impression as a professional when she looked like a refugee from Little League camp?

With a thick, heavy brush, she stroked her auburn hair furiously, then, with one quick, fluid motion, pulled her locks back away from her face and fastened them securely with a fistful of clips and one large rubber band from her desk. Next, she pulled a team cap down over her ears and surveyed her reflection once more.

She groaned. The effect was even worse. How on earth had she gotten into this situation? Why in heaven's name had she let the guys talk her into playing?

She knew the answer to that one. It was her own fault. After her brash threat to play every position herself, the guys had taken her at her word and insisted that she participate in the charity event.

"Hey, if we have to play, *you* have to play. After all, you're the one who got us into this." With this playful guilt trip, Gibby had scored his desired effect.

Now, here she was, thoroughly unprepared for her dramatic return to the baseball diamond. She hadn't played competitively in years. She hadn't even been working out consistently. What if she dropped the ball? What if she choked? What if she humiliated herself in front of hundreds of fans—and, worst of all, Tucker Boyd?

Wiping a bead of perspiration from her upper lip, she turned away from the mirror and strode purposefully toward the door.

Staring at yourself isn't going to help matters, Casey, she scolded herself. *It doesn't matter what you look like. It doesn't matter if you let people down. You just do your best. If they don't like it, that's their problem. Keep your head high and give it all you've got. After all, that's the most anyone can do.*

As she stormed out of the bathroom, she nearly ran into her team's best catcher, Walter Ojeda.

"Casey, you won't believe this!" he said, his face a mask of shock and wonder.

"What is it?"

He shook his head. "Come here. You've got to see it for yourself."

Oh, no! What now? Casey thought as she followed him outside, trying to imagine what unforeseen disaster had transpired. *I suppose the hot dog machine exploded, starting a fire that is even now consuming the concession stand.*

But to her delight—and then horror—the source of Ojeda's amazement was not some wild calamity, but rather the massive crowds that had already begun to pour into the stands. The ballpark seated over 2,600, but she'd been convinced that between the last-minute planning and the Wednesday night schedule they'd be lucky to get a thousand spectators.

"Wh—What?" Casey tripped on her tongue. "Where are they all *coming* from?"

She knew that the event had been promoted on local radio and TV stations. Even some of the Portland stations had picked up on the charity game. Yet she never would have anticipated this kind of response.

"Excuse me?" She reached out and plucked at the sleeve of an older woman who was making her way toward the stands with two little boys in tow.

"Yes?" the woman looked confused for a moment as she took in Casey's unusual attire. Then understanding struck her. "Oh! You're *her*. The owner lady! K. C., isn't it?" she said, emphasizing the last syllable of the name.

"That's right. *Ca*-sey," she responded. But before she had the opportunity to ask any questions, the woman began to gush.

"Oh, dear, we're so glad you're here. This is such a *good* thing you're doing. I know it's hard for children these days." She threw a maternal look in the direction of the two boys who had wandered several feet away. "My son is raising his boys on his own, and it isn't easy. I know if they ever got into trouble, I'd want someone to help them the way you and—" Her eyes flickered toward her grandkids. "Boys! Now you wait for Grandma! I told you—" She gave Casey an apologetic look. "Kids!" she said, then scurried away.

A dumbfounded Casey stared after them. Before she even had time to collect her thoughts, however, she was approached by a scruffy, long-haired man in his early thirties, wearing worn boots, holey jeans, and a faded black T-shirt bearing the name of a popular heavy metal band from the eighties.

"You the owner chick?" he asked abruptly.

"Uh...yes." Casey wasn't especially thrilled about being called a chick, but it was clear what the man was asking.

He nodded in appreciation. "How's The Gord?"

Casey looked at him in surprise. "'The Gord'? You...you mean Gordon Olson?"

"Yup."

She eyed him suspiciously. "Do you *know* him?"

The man shook his head. "Don't know him. Knowed *about* him, though, fer years. He wuz one of my dad's favorite ballplayers before he went and got to be a coach. They called 'im The Gord, you know. My dad always said it wuz cuz he was shaped all squashy-like."

"Really?" Casey tried to process this bit of information.

"So how's he doin'?" the man pushed.

Looking into his eyes, past his rough manner, Casey could see that he really cared.

"He's stable," she said kindly. "He's going to have to have angioplasty this week, but that's pretty normal after a heart attack like the one he had. He's got a long way to go yet, but they say he should be just fine."

"Good!" the man said vehemently, sloshing the drink he held in his hand.

"Is that why you came tonight?" Casey asked. "Because of Gordon?"

"Yup," the man confirmed, then turned to walk away. "Just wanted to give my support," he threw over his shoulder. "Let the ol' Gord know we wuz thinkin' 'bout 'im."

Casey watched, incredulously, as the odd man disappeared into the crowd.

"This is unbelievable," she said to Ojeda, who was still standing beside her. The fans continued to pour in. Then the thought hit her: in less than fifteen minutes, she would be catching in front of this crowd.

113

"Umm...you know, it's not too late for me to back out," she suggested hopefully. "You and Daly can have the glory all to yourselves!"

"Oh, no you don't," Ojeda laughed and pulled on her arm. "You're not going anywhere. We'll be catching all season. Tonight, we're *more* than happy to share the spotlight with you." Casey continued to drag her feet as he herded her toward the field. "Besides, I wouldn't miss this for the world!"

Casey reached into the stack of bats and pulled out a good-sized Louisville, her favorite. Instinctively, she grabbed the bat with her left hand and wound up her right arm in one last, sweeping windmill swing, although she didn't need to. She'd stretched so much while waiting for her turn at bat, she was already beginning to feel like Gumby.

With lightning-quick glances, she surveyed the situation: The score was tied 2-2 at the bottom of the third. On the pitcher's mound, Gibby waited for Daly's signal. With two outs, she had two runners in scoring position: Barrientos at first base and Niemeyer on third. From his position one base away, the six-foot-two blond chomped furiously on a wad of gum, then, catching her eye, grinned and winked.

Casey took a deep breath.

She had a lot to prove. It was true that she was gradually gaining respect with the coaches, but Shelton was still furious about her firing Hatch. And although the players' esteem for her seemed to be growing, there were a few members of the team who still questioned her level of expertise.

Casey suspected that there were also members of the public who remained unconvinced of her abilities. When she'd first inherited the team, news reporters had called the fledgling sportscaster everything from a "lucky heiress" to a "glorified weather girl." The memory made her cringe.

There were, no doubt, people in the stands who'd heard she'd be playing and had come to see her fail. Like onlookers at the scene of an accident, spectators were simply drawn to…well, *spectacles*. And as the only woman in a game with twenty-five professional ballplayers, Casey knew that she was the biggest spectacle of them all.

Carefully, she kicked the excess dirt from her cleats and placed her feet in position.

Her eyes roved the stands above right field…and were caught by the sight of a large cardboard sign, sloppily printed with the words: GET WELL COACH.

Casey hesitated, then stepped out of her stance and glanced toward left field. Up in the bleachers, she spied a second sign: WELCOME BACHELORS—TO OUR PAD! The letters blurred as her eyes misted over with tears.

Suddenly, all thoughts about her own performance, and all fears about how she was perceived by the public, disappeared. And as she made this conscious decision, for the first time she was able to hear the faint roar of the crowd.

Casey slipped off her batting helmet, and the thunder of applause grew louder in her ears. Tossing the DiMarini onto the ground, she threw both arms up in the air, grinned like a maniac, and began waving furiously as the cheering rose to a crescendo.

To Casey, time seemed to stand still, and she drank in the beauty of the moment. Finally, after several minutes of basking in the thunderous applause, she returned to home plate, reenergized and ready to play. Again, she tapped her cleats, resumed her position, turned to the pitcher's mound…and found herself staring into the smiling hazel eyes of "Big Time" Boyd.

Casey smirked and slipped her batting helmet back over her head. She should have known Tucker would insist on pitching to her. And unless she was mistaken, he wouldn't be treating this as a slow-pitch game. *Well, I'll just have to show him what Casey Foster's got....*

She dug one cleated toe into the dirt and raised the bat in the air like a warrior's club.

The smile dropped from Tucker's face as he raised both hands overhead, drew them close to his chest, pulled back, and released.

Casey saw the pitch coming, swung, and....

"Steeee-rike one!" the umpire bellowed.

Casey blinked. She'd figured Boyd would hold back a bit and half-expected a slider. The fastball he'd popped over the outer half of the plate had taken her completely by surprise.

What's the matter with you, Casey? she grumbled to herself. *You had no business swinging at that! You've got a runner ready to come in. Don't get overanxious now. Wait for a good one. Wait...*

Tucker wound up again. His next pitch was low and inside, and Casey pulled back just in time.

"Ball one!" cried the umpire.

Feeling more confident, she stepped back into place, raised her bat a little higher, and prepared to wipe that grin off Tucker's face once and for all.

She waited. She watched Tucker wind up. And then, he made the mistake of sending her another heater—right down the middle. The sheer speed of his first pitch had almost frightened her. This time, however, she was ready for it, and her connection was right on the mark.

Thunderous applause erupted from the stands as Casey threw down her bat, slipped into her home-run trot, and triumphantly danced her way around the bases as Tucker Boyd looked on, wearing an expression of bewildered amazement.

～～～

Tucker tightened his grip on the bat in his hands. "I suppose you think you're hot stuff now, huh?" He threw the comment over his left shoulder at the catcher behind him.

"'Hot stuff' is such a relative term," a masked Casey joked. "Hitting a crowd-pleasing home run with two runners on base…well, it takes a pretty incredible ballplayer to do that." Out on the diamond, Heath and Esposito waited at second and third. "Not everyone is up to the challenge," she said meaningfully.

"If you're trying to distract me, you can forget it. I have nerves of steel and the concentration of a brain surgeon," Tucker bragged.

"Oh, really?" Casey asked, as he slid her a sidelong glance. "Well, then…LOOK OUT!" She threw herself to the side, as if to escape a wild pitch.

Flinching automatically, Tucker dropped his bat and leaped out of the way.

As the crowd began to howl, Casey leaped to her feet. "Gotcha!" she cried smugly.

With a look of disgust, Tucker leaned over and retrieved his bat, then gripped it hard, to control the shaking in his arms. "Very, very funny. You know, guys get hit by balls all the time. It really isn't something to joke about."

"You're right, I'm sorry." Casey managed to bring her laughter under control. "It's just that…WHOA!" Again, she ducked. And again, Tucker fell for it. By this time, not only the crowd, but the entire team was in stitches.

"Yeah, yeah, yeah." Tucker turned back toward the mound and focused on relief pitcher Eddie Cage. "Well, we're in our last inning, and I'm about to slam this ball out of the park. We'll just see who's laughing in about three minutes."

"Oooooh, I'm scared," Casey pretended to tremble.

She prepared to give Eddie the signal. But what should she call? A knuckleball? A curve? She licked her dusty lips in anticipation. No, she had Boyd rattled now. A heater would be ideal. All she had to do was give a little giggle, and he'd be completely off the mark. Of course, some people might not consider such a strategy very sporting. But then, she didn't remember reading anything in the official rule book that forbid giggling behind the batter.

Casey knelt and, lowering her mask over her face, dropped the signal—one finger between her legs.

Eddie nodded, touched two fingers to the bill of his cap, and sent one in hard and fast....

And Tucker annihilated it.

Casey groaned as the ball flew into the narrow gap in left center, looking graceful and pale, like a bird in flight.

Out in left field, Herberto Lainez took off after it, running as if his life depended on making the catch.

By the time Casey looked down, Tucker had already rounded first base and was headed for second. Shouting like a victorious warrior, Cody Heath pounded across home plate, scoring the opposing team's third run. In the distance, Lainez snagged the ball as Esposito charged in for a fourth.

Tucker had cleared second and was almost to third base when Steinkamp caught Lainez's throw and drilled it toward Casey.

The throw was off, but not by much. Casey threw her mask to the ground. Then, hollering "I got it! I GOT IT!" at the top of her lungs, she took several giant steps to the right, caught the ball neatly in her glove, spun on her left foot, and threw herself at home plate.

Apparently having underestimated Casey's ability to catch the ball, Tucker was making a bold attempt to run across the base. Too late to slide, he realized that he was about to be tagged and, letting out a great cry, he threw himself in the air, making one last, desperate attempt at a winning play.

Casey took one final, giant step back and planted her foot onto home plate, directly where Boyd's foot was headed. Then, leaning forward as the enormous figure came flying toward her, she reached out to make the tag.

And everything went black.

13

Injuries are part of the game. Without them, I wouldn't have a job.
GENE GIESELMANN, ST. LOUIS CARDINALS TRAINER, 1987

Casey reached into the freezer and pulled out her second—and final—ice tray. She'd been home less than an hour-and-a-half, and already she'd melted twelve cubes on her ballooning lower lip.

Carefully, she wrapped four more frosty squares in a soft terry washcloth, refilled the bright blue tray, and prayed that God would miraculously speed up the ice-making process. The way her mouth was throbbing, she'd be lucky if she got any sleep at all tonight, and there was simply too much to do for her to miss work tomorrow.

Not that she wouldn't do so in a heartbeat if responsibilities allowed. Casey closed her eyes and tried to imagine what it would be like at the park in the morning. The guys had always loved tormenting her. Now, they were certain to be merciless. She could hear it already: "You know, Casey...it's not that we don't think you know that much about the game...but we really don't think baseball is supposed to be a full-body contact sport." The fact that Tucker had been declared "Safe!" only added to her humiliation.

At first, the players had been sympathetic, compassionate,

and concerned. But when the extent of the injuries turned out to be a bruised lip and a bump on Casey's head, and a black-blue-and-purple eye for Boyd, the snickering and teasing had quickly reached full swing, as in: "Hey, Boyd! Looks like you and Casey are really *falling* for each other!" and "Casey, I was wondering if you could give me a few tips on how to tag someone out? Nothing big. A simple *crash* course will do!"

The media had been thrilled. And judging by the comments from the local sports reporter, Casey was going to hit the late news as the funniest personality to hit baseball since Yogi Berra.

Kicking back against the soft comfort of her pale peach Cambridge sofa, Casey held the ice-filled washcloth to her lip with one hand and reached for the remote control with the other.

"Might ath well get thith ober with," she lisped grumpily, switching to the ten o'clock news.

After nearly ten minutes of reports about local forestry issues and community events, Casey was ready to breathe a sigh of relief. Nothing had been mentioned. Maybe the news department hadn't found the event to be airworthy after all. Although that seemed unusual, considering the promotion they had given it during the previous weeks....

"And stay tuned for highlights of tonight's charity baseball game between the new Bend Bachelors...and the new Bend Bachelors! And find out why we're not kidding when we say, this team's owner and star player are a real *hit!*"

Casey groaned and buried her head under one of her soft throw pillows. *Oh, good grief. This is going to be worse than I thought.*

When a knock sounded on the door, she decided it was the perfect end to a disastrous evening. *Great. Here I am, wearing my grungiest sweats, with my lip swollen to twice its normal size. I need a shower. I'm not wearing any makeup. And now I have a surprise visitor. Not to mention the fact that I'm about to be humiliated on television. Does it get any better than this?*

A quick look through the peephole revealed that her visitor was, indeed, a big surprise.

Tucker Boyd.

Casey pulled her face away from the small glass opening and stopped for a moment to collect her thoughts. The last she had seen of Tucker, he was being led away by trainer Herb Madsen, who was mumbling something about a "stupid risk" for a "ridiculous charity game." It was bad enough that she'd been consumed by guilt. No doubt the two of them had had a heyday ripping her to pieces for her careless mistake.

She set her lips in a determined line. No! Playing that game was not a mistake. It had been a fluke accident. And if he was here to chew her out, she would simply tell him so. Still, despite her best efforts, Casey's feeling of regret would not be completely squelched.

The rapping resumed, and Casey timidly reached up on tiptoe and peered through the glass once more. This time, she was met by the disconcerting image of one large eye pressed up against the peephole.

She laughed heartily and, keeping the washcloth pressed to her lips, unhooked the deadbolt latch and opened the door.

At the sight of Casey and her homemade ice pack, Tucker looked both amused and chagrined. *His* eye, she noticed, was swelling up nicely and rivaled her lip as the ugliest injury of the night.

"Boyd?" Before she could stop herself, she'd blurted out: "What are you doing here?"

"Nice to see you, too," he said dryly. "May I come in?" His eyes scanned the room behind her, taking in the rich, thick, chocolate brown carpet, authentic hardwood paneling, and clean white walls. A soft green afghan lay strewn across the couch where she had been lying. From its position along the far wall at her left, the small, color Mitsubishi television blared out an irritating, yet catchy cat food jingle—the kind she hated to watch, but could not help humming for a week after she'd heard it.

"Well…" Casey hesitated, one hand flying automatically to her unkempt hair. "It'th pretty late." *What am I doing?* she thought. *It doesn't matter how I look. I'm his boss, not his girlfriend.*

At the sound of her lisp, Tucker laughed. "I won't stay long," he assured her with a twinkle in his eye.

"Uh…I thuppoth that'th all right." She stepped back and allowed him to enter. It was only then that she noticed he was carrying a large, brown grocery sack.

"Thtopping by on your way home from the thtore, I thee?"

"Actually, I was just—oh, look! It's us!"

Casey followed his gaze. Sure enough, there they were on television, big as life, in a promotional shot that had been filmed in the ballpark before the game.

They both moved into the living room and sank down on the sofa to watch what they knew was coming.

At the right of the frame, Casey stood between Gibby and Cortez, playfully assuming the role of peacemaker as the two staged a mock fight as representatives of the "opposing" teams. In the background, the rest of the players laughed and joked among themselves, while a few, including Boyd, looked on in amusement. Upon closer inspection, however, Casey saw that his eyes were trained not on his comical teammates, but on Casey herself. And the look in his eyes was one that could only be described as "tender."

The news piece shifted to a live shot of a vivacious blonde reporter standing in front of the stadium. "The event was sponsored and staged by the Bend Bachelors, just two days before their own opening day, as a fund-raiser for a local nonprofit youth program—"

"Thith ith *not* going to be good," Casey said warily.

"Now, now," Tucker clucked at her. "Don't be a spoilsport. Remember, this is for *charity*."

"Watch it, buthter. I'll give *you* charity," she threatened.

"—the final moments of the game," the perky blonde was saying, "when former superstar Tucker Boyd scored the winning run, triggering a chain of events that resulted in the flattening of catcher—and team owner—Casey Foster at home plate."

As the woman spoke, the events in question unfolded on the screen. Casey watched with great interest as the camera showed her leaping into the air like a crazed ballerina, turning, then setting her foot on home base as Tucker propelled through the air. When final contact was made, she checked the placement of her foot.

"Did you thee that? Did you *thee* that?" Casey jumped off the couch. "I knew it! I *had* you. You know I did!"

"Hmmm," Tucker settled back against the couch, revealing no emotion. "We see what we want to see," he told her seriously.

Casey bounced on the cushions beside him. "What? You've got to be kidding! You can't tell me that you—"

With more than a little amusement, he watched her spring up and down. "All right! *May*-be—and I'm just saying *maybe* here—you might have tagged me. But that's beside the point now—"

"What do you mean, it'th bethide the point?" Casey sputtered. "I *thaw* you—"

"Yes, and I saw *you*," he said, with a hint of accusation in his voice.

Casey stopped bouncing and opened her eyes wide. "What? What did I do?"

Tucker raised one eyebrow. "Are you kidding?" He pointed dramatically to his eye. "You didn't do this with just that dainty little hand of yours."

"What do you mean? You aren't thaying that I hit you with the—"

"That's right," he said a bit smugly. "You used that nice, sweet little fist of yours to cram a baseball into the eye of your favorite pitcher."

"Oh!" Casey felt momentarily guilty. Then she eyed him suspiciously. "Are you thure you're not jutht making that up?" she said, sounding like she didn't believe him. "And by the way, who ever thaid you were my favorite pitcher?"

Boyd kicked his feet up on her antique-chest coffee table. "I can just tell," he said smugly.

"Yeah?" Casey refused to get pulled in by his charm. "Well, we believe what we want to believe—"

"All right," he grinned, an action that sent a tiny shiver of delight down Casey's spine. "Enough sparring for one night. I came not to wage war, but to make peace."

"Oh?" She eyed him doubtfully. "And how do you ekthpect to do that?"

Tucker stood up and walked over to the bag he had deposited on the floor, then carried it to the counter of her kitchenette, which was actually a part of the large "great room."

"I come bearing relief supplies," he said. As he spoke, he reached into the sack, pulled out each item, and laid it on the other kitchen counter. "Let's see, we have Band-Aids…ice, and…ah, yes! Chocolate." He beamed at Casey's cry of appreciation.

"I didn't know that chocolate maketh you heal better!"

"It doesn't," he admitted. "I just figure that if you're going to be miserable, you might as well enjoy it." He continued to rummage in the depths of the bag. "Oh, and one more thing. Ta-da!" Triumphantly, he pulled out a thin, plastic-wrapped package.

"What'th that?" Casey said warily.

"A steak!"

"A thteak? Ithn't it a little late for dinner?"

"Silly woman," Tucker shook his head disapprovingly. "It's not to eat. It's purely for medicinal purposes. I remembered that when I was a kid, I saw Peter put a steak on his face when he hurt himself on *The Brady Bunch*."

Casey rolled her eyes. "That'th for a *black eye*, Tucker. You don't really ekthpect me to walk around with a raw thteak on my *lip*? That'th dithguthting. And highly unthanitary."

"Hmmm. Good point." He stood with his hand poised over the bag, deliberating. "Oh, well…guess *I'll* just have to use it then!"

Casey watched in surprise as he unwrapped the package and slapped the moist slab of red meat on his bruised face.

"*Ugh!* I think I'm going to be thick." She sank back into the cushions, clutching her stomach.

"Good!" Abandoning his treasures on the counter, Tucker came to sit beside her, casually laying one well-muscled arm along the back of the sofa. "At least you're not thinking about your lip anymore."

She continued to face forward, trying to ignore the nearness of his arm. Although there were several inches between his hand and her back, she imagined she could feel the warmth of his touch.

"My *fat* lip you mean," she said, finally looking at him. "The one I have *you* to thank for."

"Me?" he said innocently, arching his eyebrows.

"Don't look at me like that. Yeth, *you*," she scolded. "I think you did thith on purpoth."

"Like you *meant* to smash my eye?"

"Well…all right," Casey allowed. "Maybe it *wath* an acthident. Even if you did get called thafe. How'd you do that anyway? Bribe the ump?"

Tucker puffed up his chest. "Well, when you're a great, big, brute of a man, like I am—"

"Thtop!" Casey giggled and smacked him on the top of the head with one of her cream-colored throw pillows. "You're thuch a goofball—"

"The term is 'idiot'," Tucker corrected her. "Remember? You told the team that only an idiot could get hurt at a charity ball game."

She began to shake with laughter. "Oh!" she groaned. "And you and I have got to be the biggetht idiotth of them all."

"The very worst!" Tucker agreed, watching her in amusement. But Casey's mirth was contagious. Pretty soon, his own shoulders began to shake, and the two of them laughed—great, rolling belly laughs—until the tears poured down their faces and they were clutching their stomachs.

"Oh, my!" Casey finally said, wiping the tears from her eyes. "That'th the betht laugh I've had thinth—" She sniffled, sobering. "Well, before Uncle Edward died."

Tucker reached over and brushed away a lock of unruly hair that had fallen over her eyes. Then he drew his hand softly along her cheek in a gesture of tenderness. "You miss him very much, don't you?"

Casey nodded wordlessly, her mirth forgotten at the sudden reminder of her loss.

"Yeah." Tucker's deep hazel eyes searched hers. Then, without warning, he leaned forward and folded her into a gentle embrace.

At first, Casey stiffened, shocked by the unexpected show of compassion. Then, without thinking, she began to relax, and allowed herself to simply rest against the comfort of Tucker's strong, muscular shoulder.

Neither spoke.

For a moment, time stood still.

Then Casey stirred. Her heart beat wildly as she inhaled the spicy scent of soap and masculinity that was uniquely Tucker Boyd. The fragrance was heady, and she closed her eyes as if to block it from her mind—but the loss of one sense simply made the others more intense. Casey heard him draw a ragged breath, felt the gentle touch of his fingers against her arms....

She blinked. This was impossible! Hadn't she already determined that she could not fall for this man? Not once since their first discussion of the subject had he mentioned anything about his relationship with God. His attendance at the weekly prayer meetings was sporadic, and often he did not pray—at least not aloud—when he did attend. Casey could not allow herself to be drawn in by a man who did not love God. Nor would she fall into the trap of 'missionary dating.' That was just playing with fire.

Casey cleared her throat and rose to her feet, and Tucker let his hands fall away without protest. "Did I hear you thay you brought ithe? That'th great becauth—oh, brother! Look at thith...I've melted my ithe pack all over mythelf." She pretended to show great interest in the wet spot on her knee. "My mom alwayth thaid, make *thure* you keep ithe on it, Cay-they. I wath kind of a tomboy, tho I got hurt a lot ath a kid."

She prattled on about everything—and nothing—as she moved into the kitchen and scurried about, while trying to avoid Tucker's eyes.

"Here." Tucker moved to help her as she struggled with the thick plastic bag of ice. "Let me get that."

Before she could protest, he grabbed it from her hands and opened it with one hard pull.

"Thankth," she said, feeling uncharacteristically helpless.

"Now, let's get you fixed up." Boyd grabbed a fistful of cubes and folded them into the cloth in Casey's hands. Tucking in the corners, he raised it to her lip.

"Wait a minute." He stopped and looked at her injury more closely. "That's not just a bruise. You've got a pretty nasty cut there, too. Did you put anything on it?"

She shrugged. "No, I jutht—"

"Come here," he commanded, digging into the bag once more.

"But—"

"Don't argue." His voice was firm.

With a dramatic sigh, she stepped close and submitted to his ministrations.

"You know, you're pretty good at thith, Tucker Nightingale," she teased. *A little too good.* "I—uh—thuppothe you've had a lot of practith?" She was fishing, and she knew it.

Tucker looked amused. "At which part?" he asked, popping open a bag of cotton balls. "Getting injured, or playing doctor?"

"Boyd!" She clamped her lips together primly. "Ouch! No, I mean—that ith—" She was thoroughly flustered now. "It'th jutht that, well…you're much gentler than I would have imagined." At exactly that moment, one massive hand was delicately dabbing a bit of Bactine on her lip.

"Maybe you bring out the best in me," he whispered softly.

Slowly, instinctively, Casey leaned forward and reached up with long, slim fingers to gently touch the angry bruise around Tucker's eye. Her breath caught in her throat and her heart pounded as he bent forward slightly and drew her close, then began to lower his lips toward hers.…

"Tucker, wait." She laid one hand against his chest and pulled back.

"What is it?" He looked at her in confusion.

"I…can't." Her eyes implored him to understand.

"But I thought—you seemed to—" He dragged one hand across his stubbled chin.

"I know. But…thith jutht ithn't right."

129

"You could have fooled me." He sounded frustrated. Casey turned away, not wanting to see the anger in his eyes. He reached out and grabbed her arm, gently but firmly. "Are you saying that you're not interested? That you don't feel anything?"

Not interested? How could she say that? For weeks, he had completely consumed her thoughts. Not feel anything? Already she felt more for him than she had felt for any man she'd ever known.

"I *need* to know," he insisted, his expression grave. "What is it? What's the matter?"

Casey bit back the words she so desperately wanted to speak. *Of course I feel something for you. Every day, I look forward to the moment I first see you…to seeing your face light up when our eyes meet across the room. To watching the excitement, the passion on your face as you face one physical challenge after another. But, Tucker…I can't be in a relationship with a man who doesn't truly love God. And I don't want you to make a decision to follow him simply because it's what I expect or need.…*

The realization hit her. She could not tell him the truth. If Tucker knew her reasons, he might very well decide to pursue a relationship with God, then later abandon that decision, just as he had in college. She needed to know that his commitment was sincere—and one that would last.

"Thith…jutht ithn't what I want," she said flatly. She could not speak the words with conviction. Her only hope was to keep all signs of emotion from her voice. "I'm thorry."

Tucker's mouth fell open a fraction, as if he could not believe what he had just heard, and Casey watched in horror as a dark expression of pain passed over his eyes. "I'm sorry, too," he said finally, then turned and strode purposefully across the room.

Without even pausing, he wrapped his hand around the classic gold doorknob and pulled hard, swinging the door open with far more force than was necessary.

"Tucker, wait!" Casey cried, taking a step after him.

He paused only long enough to throw one last glance over his shoulder, offering an icy, "Good-night."

Long after he had gone, Casey continued to stare at the spot where she had last seen him. And suddenly, her greatest hurt wasn't the pain in her lip.

It was the ache in her heart.

~ 14 ~

*The last time I saw anything like this, I was playing for
Tastee Freeze in the Little League.*

Dave Smith, Houston Astros pitcher, on falling
behind Cincinnati 14-0 after one inning, 1989

FRIDAY, MAY 16—OPENING DAY

"Cue Barry Bachelor! Cue the clown! Where is he? Oh! Thank
goodness!" Casey watched in relief as the team mascot ran
onto the field and started jitterbugging to the beat of
Deniece Williams's 1980s hit, "Let's Hear It for the Boys," blaring over the public address system.

The crowd roared in appreciation, and Casey let out a huge
sigh of relief. After weeks of long, hard effort, opening day had
finally arrived. The guys were already in the dugout, fairly
chomping at the bit. And with the exception of a few, minor
snags, the pregame promotions had so far been a tremendous
success.

The entire event had begun with a heartwarming parade by a
crowd of energetic Little Leaguers, followed by an enthusiastic, if
not well choreographed, performance by a marching band from
one of the local high schools. Trombones, trumpets, flutes, and
clarinets—all rang out in their own keys, belting out a sad rendition of "Louie, Louie," which Casey considered to be the most
overused song ever played by high school bands. However,

when the confused tuba player accidentally staggered off the field, and the audience enthusiastically cheered out directions like spectators at a game of pin-the-tail-on-the-donkey, Casey decided that she'd have to ask the out-of-step teens to return again...and soon.

After the marching band meandered off the field, the mayor of the city made a dramatic, perfectly timed entrance by helicopter, and the crowd had listened patiently as he delivered a brief introductory welcome to the new double-A team. And now, Casey hoped, the mascot she'd hired would whip the crowd back into a frenzy just in time for the first inning.

Out on the field, Barry Bachelor continued to skip about to the music. Casey laughed at the sight. Ross Chambers, the acrobat she'd hired, was dressed in a full-body costume that made him look like an enormous puppet. The entire getup was ridiculous, but it was the head—the enormous, silly, felt head—that drew the most attention.

At least four sizes bigger than a normal person's cranium, the big, round dome featured a bright red, smirking mouth, a bulbous nose, and huge plastic eyes, with black pupils that jiggled and bounced as the creature walked. Planted on top was a stylish top hat the size of a large microwave oven.

The mascot's body was dressed in a dapper tuxedo, and he twirled a baseball bat like a cane as he ran through the stands, flirting outrageously with the female spectators.

The crowd loved it.

Casey glanced at her watch. It was almost game time.

She ran to the dugout.

"Okay, guys, front and center!" A few of the players straggled over and gathered around her. "Daly? Vazquez? Espo? Gibby?" Come on, all you guys." The remaining players reluctantly tore their eyes away from the field and joined the group. Casey didn't blame them for being distracted. They'd been waiting a long time for this moment, and for many, this would be their first professional game. Expectations and emotions were running high.

"All right, I already gave you a pep talk, and so did Dutchie. You're ready," she said. "But before we start, I want to take a moment to give this game over to God." Before she closed her eyes, she noticed that the men seemed to be willingly bowing their heads.

"Lord, thank you for this day," Casey began. "Thank you for being here with us. Please be with us in the hours ahead. Keep us free from injuries, and keep us honest. Help us to play with our deepest, truest love for the game. We trust the results to you. Amen.

"And now…" she continued as the players looked up at her expectantly, "let's play ball!"

With a great battle cry, the men ran for the stairs and headed up toward the field. Before Tucker could blend in with the crowd, Casey reached and clutched at his arm. He had managed to avoid her all afternoon, and now his eyes were stormy.

"How are you doing?" she asked carefully.

"My arm's fine." Tucker's voice was devoid of emotion. He looked over his shoulder as the other men disappeared onto the field.

"I'm not worried about your arm. I want to know how *you* are doing." She resisted the urge to reach out and run gentle fingers along the hard set of his jawline.

"Nothing for you to worry about. I've gotta get out there." He turned and ran after the other players.

There was nothing Casey could do but watch him go.

With the exception of Wednesday night's fiasco, Tucker Boyd hadn't played before a crowd in nearly two years. Despite the small size of the crowd—twenty-six hundred fans as opposed to the thousands to which he had become accustomed—Tucker found the welcome warm and friendly, and the sound of cheering voices filled his ears like a song.

At the plate, Martin Ruger, the Pioneers' leadoff man, threw Tucker a look of challenge. The message struck him like a lightning bolt. The guy didn't think he could do it! Ruger probably figured he was on his way down. First double-A, then single...then back to Wisconsin and a factory job. Well, he'd show him—he'd show all of them—that Tucker Boyd wasn't ready for retirement...not yet.

Ojeda called the pitch. Two fingers. The catcher was looking for a curve. Tucker shook his head and signaled back with one swipe down his thigh. Subtract one. He was going for the heat.

Tucker wound up, released a strong, powerful pitch...and missed, high and outside.

"Ball one!"

As Ruger adjusted his stance, Ojeda crouched and threw one fist between his knees, pretending to give a signal, while shaking his head.

Picking up on the faked shake-off, Tucker waggled his head in return, hoping that Ruger would overthink and get psyched out, then watched as Ojeda threw him the real signal. Three fingers.

Nice. A slider. His most effective inside pitch against right-handed batters. Tucker knew he'd be much more likely to get a strike with a slider than with a curve or a split-finger fastball. Not as much of a challenge, but, hey...a strike was a strike, and a better way to start the game than with another outside call.

Boyd stepped into position, raised his arms, wound up, and

let go a beautiful backdoor slider that caught the outside edge almost perfectly...but also caught too much of the plate. Helplessly, he watched as Ruger's bat connected with the ball, sending it high into the air.

Tucker looked toward the dugout, where Casey stood between Dutchie and Herb. And at the sight of her disappointed face, his heart dropped lower than a sinking fastball.

Casey sat at the end of the dugout bench, her head in her hands. How in the world had this happened? The evening had begun with such a powerful, rousing start.

And then the team took the field.

The bad luck had started with poor Tucker. Casey's heart ached as she remembered the look on his face when Ruger nailed his slider. But that was just the beginning of the bloodbath. By the middle of the fourth inning, Boyd had given up seven runs and eleven hits—including two home runs that put the game well out of the Bachelors' reach, even before it was half over. Dutchie had been forced to send in Gibby, taking Boyd out of the game. Tucker hadn't spoken since.

The one bright spot in the game had been shortstop John Cortez, who'd played like a consummate professional—raising Casey's credibility even further in the eyes of her players.

But Tucker...poor Tucker. He'd seemed confident enough. Perhaps too confident. The look in his eyes when he'd faced down Ruger had been one of grim determination and angry pride. His obsession with winning had not faded. If anything, his long absence from competition seemed to have sharpened his hunger for victory.

Casey watched as the spectators filed solemnly from the ballpark. Disgruntled fans had started to leave as early as the fourth inning, and by the seventh-inning stretch the stands had been half empty. Nine to three had been the final score. *At least the pregame show was a hit,* Casey reminded herself, trying to find a bright spot in the evening. But a quick glance around the field revealed that even Barry Bachelor and the out-of-step marching band were long gone.

Yet, despite the brutal disappointment, Casey found herself feeling a sense of...was it relief? It wasn't that she'd wanted Tucker to do poorly. On the contrary, she'd been praying for him all week. Still, she couldn't help but feel thankful that there didn't seem to be much chance of him hitting his stride in the near future and being called back to the big leagues.

The realization hit her like a ton of bricks. What a horrible thing to think! How selfish. How mean-spirited. How... human. And no matter how undesirable her thoughts might be, she knew it was important to figure out what they were all about.

She shook her head, as if to shake the emotions away and try to come to grips with what she was feeling.

She *couldn't* be glad that Tucker was staying. He was selfish. He was rude. Well...maybe he wasn't exactly rude. But he was avoiding her. Although, if the truth were told, that was probably her fault. And he wasn't really selfish. It was just the twelve-year-old Tucker inside him who still wanted more than anything in the world to win for his daddy. And he had to keep trying, no matter what it took....

No! Casey turned and began to gather up her belongings. It had been a ridiculous ball game, and this was a ridiculous train of thought. The day's events only confirmed what she had been telling herself for weeks: Tucker Boyd was not the man for her. He was arrogant, overconfident, and headed for self-destruction. No one could face the kind of disappointment, the kind of anguish he was most certainly headed for, without coming out the other side emotionally scarred. Not unless he was willing to turn his hurts over to God. But by the looks of things, Tucker was still trying to fix his life all by himself.

And if Casey was not mistaken, he was headed for a major league disappointment.

Tucker expertly maneuvered his bright red Mazda Miata through the traffic on Highway 97, headed toward his rented cabin home at the picturesque Sun River resort. Despite the fact that his arms and legs were still shaking from the adrenaline rush of playing and his intense feelings of anger, Tucker managed to keep the car under control and at a reasonable speed.

Never before have I been so totally *humiliated.* He wondered who had been the most shocked and disappointed by his performance: pitching coach Don Shelton, the small-town fans who had looked forward to having their very own major league superstar, or the one person he had wanted to please most: Casey.

None of those three, he finally decided. No one could be more appalled by his weak pitching than Tucker himself.

Unless it was his dad.

Tucker cast up a quick prayer of thanks for the fact that his father was not around to see him suffer such a terrible humiliation. Then, feeling guilty, he tried to retract it.

"Lord, I didn't mean that the way it sounded. But, then, I guess you knew that, didn't you? It's just that—" Tucker searched for the words. "It's just that I know how important it was to him that I do well. I hated letting him down." Sweaty hands gripped the steering wheel. "I *really* hate letting Casey down, too." He tried to control his thoughts, but it was as if a picture of Casey's sad face had been imprinted on his mind. Tucker blinked his eyes against the image. It only became clearer. If only he hadn't let her down! If only he could be the man she wanted him to be. The kind of man she deserved....

"Whoa! Sorry!" Tucker apologized through his side window, after very nearly swerving into the right-hand lane. The other driver was unable to hear his words, but looked across the lane and made eye contact. At first, the man's face was a mask of irritation. However, after Tucker had taken the time to mouth a second apology, recognition—and momentary pleasure—graced the man's features, before being replaced with an expression of anger.

"Guess he saw the game tonight," Tucker grumbled as he accelerated away from the other car. "So much for my adoring fans. You see what I'm up against, God?"

At one time, the practice of praying out loud might have seemed strange to him. But lately, Tucker had been feeling the need to face his fears. This was hard to do alone. He felt a deep desire to talk with someone, and God seemed the most reasonable choice.

He liked his teammates, but did not feel close enough to any one of them to share intimate details about his life. His first instinct had been to turn to Casey with his problems. But that was a potentially messy situation. Not only was she a woman to whom he was deeply attracted, she was also the owner of the Bachelors and a close friend of Phoenix Stars' manager, Al Clements. As such, she wielded a tremendous amount of power over his future. It wasn't that he didn't trust her. But when it came to issues concerning his professional career, it seemed wisest to keep Casey at arm's length.

Personal issues were another matter altogether. There was nothing Tucker wanted more than to share his heart with Casey, to feel the comforting touch of her hands on his as he confessed his greatest hurts and dreams. At first, he'd thought she wanted the same thing. The way her brilliant blue eyes sparkled when he entered the room, the way her gaze followed him in a crowd, the way she'd given him her treasured Bible and shown concern about his spiritual growth...how could he have thought that she didn't care?

He'd even been foolish enough to try to kiss her—a mistake that ranked right up there with tonight's crushing loss, making it one of the two most embarrassing moments of his life. What was it she'd said? That this wasn't what she wanted? Tucker scowled. Exactly what did that mean? As he had dozens of times before, he replayed in his mind the events that had occurred two nights ago.

He remembered the absurdly adorable way she'd tried to be tough with him, all the while voicing her chastisements with a childlike lisp. His heart warmed at the memory of her relaxing into his arms as he had reached out to comfort her. And there had been no mistaking the look of tenderness in her eyes as she had reached up with cool, soft fingers to touch his battered face....

But she had pulled away. And Tucker Boyd was not a man who was inclined to push his attentions on a woman who was not interested in him. There were plenty of women out there who would love to date him.

At that thought, he laughed to himself. Well, after tonight there were probably several hundred *less* who might be interested. But numbers didn't matter, anyway. He wasn't in that game. There was only one woman on his mind. The one woman who had just had a front-row view of his biggest failure to date.

The one woman he could not get out of his heart.

~ 15 ~

Baseball is a circus, and as is the case in many a circus,
the clowns and the sideshows are frequently more interesting
than the big stuff in the main tent.

W. O. McGEEHAN, SPORTSWRITER

FRIDAY, MAY 30

"Come on, G," Casey wheedled. "You gotta help me." From the top of her desk—her favorite seat in the office—she dangled her feet, kicking them against the metal legs below.

In the center of the room, Gordon Olson balanced his generously proportioned body on one of her small, orange plastic chairs. "No way, Casey. That's just not my thing. I'm a coach, not a salesman."

"This isn't sales, Gordy," she said. "It's *promotions.*"

"Whatever. Sales…promotions. Doesn't matter. That's way out of my league. Get yourself another assistant."

She pleaded with him with both her voice and her eyes. "Gordy, you know I can't afford a promotions manager yet, and I can't do this alone." In an effort to keep costs down, Casey farmed out as much office work as possible to accountants and other service providers. The rest of the responsibilities she tried to handle by herself. Some days, she felt like she operated in a complete vacuum. "I need your help."

"Nah." He stared longingly over her shoulder, out the window, at the practice taking place on the sun-drenched field. "I should be out there, anyway, with the team."

"Oh, no you don't!" Casey told him. "*Unh*-unh. I'm not going to let you go out there and get all excited. You're lucky I didn't send you home the instant you walked in the door. You're not even supposed to be back at the ballpark yet. You should be resting."

"Don't be silly. I'm fine!" Gordon said heartily.

"Humph." Casey folded her arms. "I don't know about that. Didn't I hear the doctor say you were banned from baseball *completely* for eight weeks?"

Gordy squirmed. "Now, Casey—"

"And even then, you're to be back only on a trial basis? Yes, I'm certain of it. I guess that's it, then." She jumped to her feet, grabbed the coach's hands in both of her own, and tried to pull him from the chair. "Off you go, back home."

"All right, all right." Gordon settled his weight on his ample posterior and refused to budge. "You win. I'll stay off the field and help you with your…whatever it is you call it."

Beaming, Casey clambered back up on her desk and crossed her legs, Indian-style. "Thank you very much. Now, this is the scoop. We've got all the regular game-night promotions planned already. You know: Family Night, Fan Appreciation Night, Stick-a-Hot-Dog-Up-Your-Nose Night.…"

"Huh…what?" The man pulled his gaze away from the window and looked at her in alarm.

"Just checking to make sure you were listening," Casey assured him, sounding overly dignified. "Now, this is the problem: We've lost momentum. The crowds are shrinking. We've had a few good games, but the numbers are still going down. What I need is one big event that will get everyone excited about the team again. It needs to be something fun. Something *crazy!*"

"Well, you're the one to plan it, then."

Casey ignored the comment. "It needs to have something to do with the name of the team. And remember, I'm already planning a Bachelor Party for the end of the season."

"Yeah, yeah. You took the easy one," the coach grumbled good-naturedly.

"Gordy!" Casey tried to sound threatening, but that was impossible where her favorite coach was concerned. It was a miracle to have him back, and she was enjoying every minute of his presence.

"Aha! I've got it! You could give away "Bachelors' buttons!" he said, sounding both surprised and pleased at his own suggestion.

"Hey, that's great, Gordon!" Casey enthused. "We can put the team logo on them and give 'em away—especially at weekend games, when the crowds are at their peak." She considered the idea for a moment. "It would be great, though, if we could tie the buttons in with something even bigger. Something *huge*. Something that would involve the entire community, like the charity game did."

She chewed on one thumbnail. "What we need is something people will be talking about for months. Something that just says Bachelors."

*Bachelors...bachelors...*Casey ran the word over and over in her mind, thinking, until at last her face lit up like a woman who had just been blessed with a vision.

"Oh, Gordy," she said. "I've got it. I've really got it!" She grabbed a legal-sized, yellow notepad from the desk and began to scribble furiously.

"Oh, this is *good*," she said, a grin spreading across her face. "This is very, very good." She lifted her eyes and regarded Gordon with an expression of delight. "And the guys are just gonna *hate* it!"

"A bachelor auction?"

"No way!"

"Oh, man, this time you have really gone over the top!"

Casey waited, arms folded, in the warm Oregon sunshine as waves of shock and disbelief rippled through the group. Her plans were finally in order, and she had purposely chosen this moment at which to tell the team about her latest scheme. As usual, the men were hot and sweaty after morning practice. All they wanted at that moment was to catch a shower and get into some clean clothes. Their level of patience was woefully low.

But so was their ability to hold out against her.

Out of the corner of her eye, she watched Tucker. For an instant she could have sworn that his lip was twitching in barely concealed amusement. But a moment later the look was gone, and his face was unreadable once again.

"No! Puh-*leeze* don't do this to us, Casey!" Niemeyer cried out dramatically, tossing his cap to the ground in disgust.

"I can't believe she'd capitalize on our...our *singleness* like that." Gibby threw one forearm theatrically across his forehead. "I...I just feel so cheap!"

Casey just smirked.

For several minutes, the complaints continued to flow like water over a falls. When the rush had died down to a grumbling trickle, she finally spoke. "I realize that you guys have had a couple of tough weeks," she said, adjusting her navy cap to better block the sun. "You've spent a lot of time on the road—"

"Yeah. And beside the road," Fretheim called out from the back of the group.

She grimaced as the men stirred restlessly. He had her there. While players in the bush leagues commonly faced less-than-ideal conditions, Casey believed that it was her responsibility to provide the men with the best resources available. Unfortunately, the "best" travel resource the team had at this point was an old, pale yellow, oddly shaped bus which the players had gamely nicknamed "The Twinkie."

The moniker had been comical—until the beginning of their first road trip. After that, the humor surrounding the bus lessened with each leg of the journey. The last straw had come just five days before, when the decrepit vehicle had lurched to the side of the road near the end of the six-day road trip, emitting columns of black smoke and leaving the Bachelors stranded three hundred miles from their next destination. After being rescued by a charter substitute, the team finally arrived at 5:45 for a 6:05 doubleheader. They lost both games: 6-1, 4-0.

"Just think," Casey suggested, trying to sound hopeful, "if the auction is a success and we get more fans to come out to the park, maybe then we can afford to buy a new bus and get rid of the Twinkie!"

"I got news for you, Casey," Ojeda said soberly. "The Twinkie is already dead."

"May she rest in peace," Ferraro quipped.

"Well, then...all the more reason to take steps toward getting a new bus!" Casey said brightly, not mentioning anything about the backup charter for which she had already signed a short-term lease. "Come on, guys. It's a great opportunity."

"Yeah, yeah, we know." Vazquez dug into his back pocket for his can of chewing tobacco. "It's a 'great opportunity to serve the community.'" He clamped the lid back on the can and shoved a dark wad into his mouth. "We been there before."

"Yes, you have," she agreed. "And with the exception of one minor mishap—" Her eyes flew to Tucker, who stood at the edge of the group, still maddeningly silent. "—it was a complete success."

"But...I'm married," right fielder Danny Holmes protested, sounding shocked. "I don't think my wife will go for the idea."

At that, the entire group began to howl with laughter. For several minutes, no one could speak. Even Holmes, who didn't quite catch the humor in what he had said, joined in with his own soft chuckles.

"Well, I should think not!" Casey said finally, wiping tears from her eyes. "Of course all the married guys are excused. But I'd like every single person on the team—and I mean every one—to participate." She dove further into the explanation with an excitement that made the timbre of her voice raise louder and higher.

"This is the plan. We'll contact every local business and get the top company brass—especially women—to attend. The entire function will be a fund-raiser for the same teen program we sponsored at the charity softball game. That way, something *really* good comes out of this, and whatever publicity comes our way is just an added bonus." Casey was gratified to see that several of the guys were beginning to look less reluctant and even seemed to be interested in what she was saying.

"But…what do we have to do with these ladies who, uh, 'buy' us?" Mark Houston asked nervously.

"Yeah. And what do we gotta do while we're parading around up there on the stage?" grumbled Vazquez.

"Well…nothing!" Casey protested. "I mean, of course you'll need to get up on the stage and walk around a bit during the bidding—you know, just have some fun with it. And then, I expect, a very nice, proper date will follow. But don't do anything you wouldn't normally do." She looked around at the group of rough-and-tumble rowdies who had become like brothers to her. "Uh…let me rephrase that: Don't do anything *I* wouldn't normally do." Again, laughter filled the air, and Casey felt a flush of pleasure. She had them in the palm of her hand.

"Gee, Casey, if you wanted to snag a date with me, you didn't have to go to all this trouble," Gibby teased. "All you had to do was come out and ask."

At the young pitcher's comment, Tucker's expression finally changed—to one of disapproval. Casey watched him out of the corner of her eye. He shifted his weight uncomfortably from one foot to the next, drew his cap down tighter over his ears, turned and stalked away.

"In your dreams, Gibby," Casey said with a satisfied smile. "In your dreams."

∼ *16* ∼

*The game is played with a round bat and a round ball, the players
run around the bases, and what goes around comes around*
FRANK WILLS, TORONTO BLUE JAYS PITCHER, 1989

FRIDAY, JULY 4

The air was heavy with the scent of juniper, and the stars
seemed to hang low in the sky as Casey stopped in her
tracks on her way from her car to the hotel banquet room.
She paused long enough to tighten the buckle of one low white
sandal, whose strap had stubbornly slipped off her heel for
what she guessed was the tenth time since leaving the house.
Then she fixed her eyes upon one particularly bright star and
whispered, "Please be with me tonight, God. I'm so nervous."

Inside, the banquet room was much the way she had left it
that afternoon. Brightly colored red, white, and blue balloons
were scattered everywhere, and large American flags hung from
every wall. Crisp, white linen tablecloths covered the sea of
large, round tables scattered throughout the gigantic hall. And
on top of each table, Casey had carefully placed a delicate can-
dle centerpiece trimmed with strings of white Christmas lights
and ribbons of red, white, blue, and gold lamé.

From above, six enormous crystal chandeliers bathed the
room with warm light, and the mouthwatering smells that

wafted from the caterer's buffet made Casey's stomach rumble. At twenty-five dollars a head just to get in, she had spared no expense.

The big difference from this afternoon was that the room was now filled with almost two hundred of Central Oregon's most prominent business executives, and tonight they were the epitome of style and grace. To Casey's surprise, nearly half of the men were in tuxedos, while the rest wore dressy business suits. But it was the women in the room—nearly 150 scheduled to attend, at last count—who commanded her attention: glamorous company presidents, chic marketing directors, elegant financial officers—all dressed in their most sophisticated finery.

"My goodness," she muttered under her breath. "I had no idea this town was such a bastion of fashion."

Casey looked down at her own choice: a flowing, knee-length creation, pale yellow with a light gray jacquard pattern and ivory silk trim. Pale white stockings covered her legs, and strappy white sandals adorned her feet. At her neck and ears she wore a simple matching set of pearls. *No sequins here,* she thought, a bit self-consciously.

In the far left corner, the string quartet she had hired was playing the last phrase of Grieg's "Two Lyric Pieces." As she made her way toward the front of the room, Casey heard the last few notes of the piece fade away, and then the four musicians slipped into the mournful strains of "None But the Lonely Heart."

She nearly laughed out loud. It was a tacky choice at a bachelor auction, but the violinist, who seemed to be in charge, appeared unaware that he might have made an inappropriate selection, and—to Casey's great relief—no one in the audience gave any sign of noticing what was being played.

"Where have you been?" Don Shelton rushed in from a side

entrance and clutched her by the arm. Behind him, the door swung open into a hallway that led to the waiting area behind the stage at the front of the hall. "We're about to start, and the guys are all basket cases!" he whispered loudly. "I think Niemeyer is going to throw up!"

"What? Oh, don't be silly. He's just being dramatic." Casey swallowed hard against her own rising nausea.

"Well, you wanted it to be a dramatic night. And you're gonna have it when he tosses his cookies all over the stage."

"Shelton! Don't be such a naysayer. Come on. Let's get this show on the road." And with one last, nervous glance at the crowd, Casey led the way down the hall.

"Ladies and gentlemen! Welcome to the first annual Bend Bachelors Independence Day Bachelor Auction!" The big-headed mascot leaped around the platform as the audience dissolved into fits of laughter.

Casey breathed a sigh of relief. After seeing all the elegant attendees, she had momentarily wondered if her decision to have Barry Bachelor serve as master of ceremonies was a wise one. But it had been too late to make any changes in the program at that stage of the game. Besides, there was no one better prepared to lead the event. So the creature was miked and sent onstage to meet his fate.

Thankfully, just like at the ballpark, Barry was a tremendous hit.

I hope he's not the only one, Casey worried from her vantage point just offstage. She tried to listen as Barry launched into a clever monologue about how the auction worked and who would receive the money raised, but her head was starting to spin. She took a gulp of air. Surrounded as she was by fourteen single Bachelors, all crowded together and straining to catch a glimpse of what was happening onstage, she was having considerable trouble catching her breath.

Of course, her problem also might be attributed to nerves. She closed her eyes and prayed. *"Oh, God. Please help me. How did I let these guys talk me into doing this? Please don't let me end up with some heavy breather, or a crazed lunatic who really hates his mother—"*

"Excited?" Tucker's breath was warm against her ear.

Casey jumped. "No," she said. "Nauseated."

She turned…and drank in the sight of him: six-foot-two-inches of cool masculine style.

While the men around him scrambled with last-minute adjustments to collars and ties, Tucker looked remarkably relaxed in his sleek black tuxedo. This, Casey could only attribute to his performance on the field. Despite his rocky start, Boyd's pitching had improved considerably in the last few games…as had his attitude in general. Yet he continued to remain a bit aloof where Casey was concerned. She could not remember the last time he had approached her to initiate a conversation.

"You look…great," she said uncertainly.

"And you—" Tucker lifted her hand to his lips. "—are a vision. I've never seen anything more beautiful in my life," he said with feeling.

Casey felt her cheeks flush and was thankful for the semidarkness. Suddenly, she was very glad that she had not shown up in sequins.

"Our first bachelor this evening is a six-foot-one, blond-haired, blue-eyed pitcher from Northridge, California, who likes scuba diving and clambakes," Barry was saying to the crowd. "His favorite color is sand. And his personal life motto is 'Give peace a chance.' Would you *puh*-leeze give a big, warm, Bachelor welcome to Mr. Mi-chael Gibson!"

Obediently, the crowd began to clap with enthusiasm. Then the polite cheering rose to frenzied shouts and hysterical laughter.

Casey looked to see what the audience found to be so amusing. "Oh, no!" she cried, but she, too, could not help but giggle at the sight of Gibby, strutting around the stage with his cummerbund pulled clear up under his armpits and his trousers cinched high up on his waist, leaving white socks poking out from beneath high-water pantlegs.

"Um, I just have one slight correction," Gibby said, grabbing the spare microphone that was provided as a backup, in case bouncy Barry caused his body mike to short out. "My personal motto, actually, is 'Give *me* a chance.'"

The audience roared, and Barry began to take offers, calling on each bidder with a point of his bat.

"Uh, I don't think I can do what Gibby's doing," Casey mumbled under her breath to Tucker.

"Hmmm. I knew there was a reason I liked you," he deadpanned.

His offhand compliment caused Casey's heart to give a little skip, but she forced herself to turn away and focus on the events taking place onstage.

Next up was Don Shelton. Casey was thrilled about the pitching coach's agreement to participate, which she considered to be her greatest triumph yet as owner of the Bachelors. Although he had complained loudly, he'd finally given in, mumbling that if the team had to do it, *he* would do it...but he wasn't going to like it.

Shelton stared at the back wall of the banquet room, trying not to make eye contact with any member of the wildly clapping crowd. With his slicked-back hair and slightly-too-big suit, he reminded Casey of a thirteen-year-old boy celebrating his bar mitzvah.

"Our next bachelor is a five-foot-eleven, silver-haired fox

who hails from Syracuse, New York. His hobbies are…working. His favorite color is Bachelor Blue. And his favorite saying is 'If at first you don't succeed…I don't want to hear about it.' Let's give it up for Mr. *Dooooooooon* Shelton!"

A beautiful white-haired woman leaped to her feet. "Thirty bucks!" she hollered enthusiastically.

"Thirty dollars? *Thirty dollars?*" Barry cried. "Are you kidding? We got $160 for Mike Gibson." But Shelton simply looked relieved that somebody, *anybody,* had bid on him. "Remember," the mascot chastised the woman, "this is for *charity.*"

"All right, then. Eighty bucks!" she offered.

The bidding continued, with one other stylishly dressed matron vying for the chance to spend the evening with the embarrassed-looking pitching coach. In the end, the first woman won with a bid of $120.

Don strutted off the stage, beaming.

"Oh, boy. There's going to be no living with him now," Casey predicted.

Tucker laid one hand on her shoulder and squeezed gently. "Yeah. And you're responsible for all this. I hope you can live with yourself," he teased.

Over the next hour, Barry disposed of eleven more bachelors. By nine o'clock, the candles were low and the catered buffet was stripped bare. Offstage, in the wings, only Tucker and Casey remained.

"Our next victi—I mean, auctionee—is a six-foot-two, hazel-eyed superstar from Beloit, Wisconsin. His hobbies are pitching no-hitters and winning pennants. His favorite color is the whites of his opponents' eyes. And his favorite phrase is 'It ain't over 'til it's over.' Would you please welcome Mr. Tucker *'Big Time'* Boyd!"

"That's me," Tucker whispered in Casey's ear. And then he was gone.

She watched, her heart in her throat, as he took the stage. The audience, which had been clapping enthusiastically all night, managed to raise the level of cheering to new heights.

Casey stepped forward and peeked around the stage curtain, hoping to get a better view.

She had imagined that by this time, the audience might have thinned out. But it looked like not a single woman had gone home early. In fact, a crowd of women had abandoned their tables and thronged around the base of the stage.

"One hundred dollars!" squealed a sultry-looking redhead in a sparkly green evening gown.

One hundred dollars? Gee whiz, lady. Cool your jets. To her dismay, Casey felt the unmistakable surge of jealousy.

"One hundred and twenty bucks!"

"One hundred forty!"

"One eighty!"

What on earth was going on? There wasn't even a pause in the bidding. Casey was struck by the thought that Tucker was lucky to be up onstage. If he were within reach, he might be snatched up in the women's clutches, like a cashmere sweater at a Bloomingdale's clearance sale.

Casey turned back to look across the banquet room. And then she saw her. Two tables back, flanked by gorgeous men, sat the most beautiful blonde she had ever seen.

The woman had a massive mane of golden curls and incredible violet eyes that were fixed directly on Boyd. And she was looking, Casey thought, like a cat who'd just spied a bowl of cream.

"I have two-ten. Two-hundred-and-ten dollars," Barry shouted. "Do I hear two-twenty?"

Casey held her breath. She saw it coming, but she could do nothing to stop it.

The woman stood. Dressed in black capri pants, classic

stacked-heel loafers, and a burgundy shirt of crushed velvet, she set a new standard for style in a room filled with sequins and silks. "Three hundred." The blonde did not need to shout; her voice commanded as much attention as the rest of her.

Casey clutched the fabric of her skirt beneath her hand. *Oh, no! This is* terrible....

No, it's not, she tried to tell herself. *You've already decided that you can't date Tucker anyway. He's not your type. He'd be a terrible spiritual match. He...he....* But no matter how hard she tried, she could not make the argument sound believable in her own mind.

So what? she thought, taking a different tack. *This doesn't mean a thing. It's just an auction. A* charity *auction. And your own idea, by the way, so stop complaining. It's perfectly innocent. She's a complete stranger. You have no reason in the world to believe that Tucker might like her.*

Casey swallowed hard. Who was she kidding? The woman was *gorgeous.*

As the audience acknowledged the woman's victory with applause, she stood, strolled over to the stage, and gracefully extended her hand to Tucker. Smiling, Casey thought, much more broadly than necessary, he reached down and took the blonde's hand between the same strong hands that had once held her own.

She turned away in disgust.

"All right, you two. That's enough of that! Save it for the date!" Barry joked.

Casey fumed. *I'm going to fire that clown.*

"And now," the emcee went on, "the moment you *guys* have all been waiting for! Our next bachelor is actually a *bachelorette,* hailing from Whittier, California. Her hobbies are playing sports and supporting local charities. She is notoriously kind to children, animals...and *men.*" As the audience laughed, Casey's anger at Ross Chambers, the man beneath the Barry Bachelor costume, subsided. "Her favorite color is white...the color of her heart." Ross's voice softened on the last words. "And her favorite song is 'Smile, and the Whole World Smiles with You.' Would you please welcome the sweetest bachelorette in the world...our very own Miss Casey Foster!"

As Casey stepped up to the stage, the strap of her sandal slipped from her heel once more, causing her to trip and perform a little hop-skip before falling against Barry Bachelor's shoulder.

"Hey, folks! I think she's falling for me!" he quipped.

"Uh...can it, Barry," Casey hissed, soft enough that only Ross could hear.

"Let the bidding begin!" The mascot's shoulders shook with laughter.

She closed her eyes, dreading what was to come. *You just had to have a bachelor auction, didn't you Casey? Well, now you're just going to have to live with the consequences.* She'd gotten herself into this mess. And now she was going to get what she deserved.

"I bid one-hundred-and-twenty-five dollars," piped up a young voice.

Casey ventured a glance. Near the center of the room stood a tall, thin man who looked to be about twenty-four years old. He was quite attractive, with a very boy-next-door look, and wore an adorably eager look on his face.

She smiled timidly. *You, see, Casey? You worried for nothing. This guy looks perfectly harmless....*

"Ah'll give yew a hundrit an' fifty for the little lady," a second voice boomed.

It was not hard to locate her second admirer. Like his voice, the man himself was enormous—both in height and girth. Even his black cowboy hat was oversized. He stood at the front of the hall, wearing a wide grin that exposed slightly yellowing teeth.

Oh, Lord. Please, no.

With a hopeful look on her face, she turned back to the young man who had started the bidding. His cheerful expression had been replaced with a scowl of discouragement, and he was carefully examining the contents of his wallet.

"One hundred and seventy," someone offered.

Casey had not even located the source of the voice when the cowboy bellowed out again.

"Two hundrit!"

Casey's heart sank. The bidding continued, but it was easy to see what the results would be. For some absurd reason, the man was determined to win her...and money appeared to be no object. Her eyes sought out Tucker.

She finally spied him, standing at the side of the room, next to the stunning blonde. The woman was talking animatedly, gesturing with pale, graceful hands as she spoke. Tucker appeared to be making an effort to listen, but it was clear that he was watching the stage carefully and was alarmed by the latest turn of events.

With her eyes, Casey begged him to save her.

Tucker froze. A look of compassion—and something else—passed over his face. Then he stepped forward, opened his lips to speak, and...

"Sold!" Barry cried out jubilantly.

Tucker's mouth snapped shut.

Casey pasted a plastic smile on her face.

Her fate was sealed.

17

The best way to avoid ballplayers is to go to a good restaurant.
TIM MCCARVER, ANNOUNCER AND FORMER CATCHER, 1987

FRIDAY, JULY 11

Hey, what's that stink?" Casey wrinkled her nose as she came into the lunchroom. She was used to being greeted with an odd bouquet of aromas at mealtime, since some of the men had quite unusual tastes. But today's smell was particularly offensive, even to her odor-tolerant nose.

"Danny's lunch," Ojeda said disgustedly, pushing his own, half-eaten meal away.

Across the table from him, the right fielder threw up his hands in protest. "What?" Holmes said innocently. "My wife made it last night. It's good."

"Yeah, but—ugh!" At the kitchenette counter, Eddie Cage put down the glass of water he had just poured and clutched at his stomach, as though he might be sick. "You didn't have to *burn* it. What did you have it in the microwave for? Eight minutes?"

"Tuna casserole, Danny?" Casey sniffed the air as she joined them at the table and opened up her own container of pasta salad. "Is that on your training diet?"

"If it is, I suggest you take it off," Tucker remarked dryly from his customary seat at the head of the long formica table.

"Ha, ha. Very funny. I suppose you—hey!" Holmes stopped and blew a wolf whistle as Don Shelton entered the room, looking more like a little boy than ever with his brand-new, close-clipped haircut. "Look at you, Shelly! Sportin' a new 'do.'"

"It's a haircut, Holmes." Don scowled and went to grab a bottle of spring water from the refrigerator. "You know, you could use one yourself."

The guys exchanged mischievous glances. "Gettin' all gussied up, are you, Shel…for your *date*?" Cage laughed.

"Shel-ly's got a *girl*-friend, Shel-ly's got a *girl*-friend," Ojeda recited in a singsong voice and waved his arms daintily in the air.

"All right, that's enough," Casey said, doing everything she could not to break up into laughter herself. The guys were entertaining enough, but Don was hilarious as he stood helplessly, trying to figure out how to deflect the men's teasing, getting redder and redder by the minute. Compassion, however, got the upper hand, and she managed to keep a smirk from her face. "Leave him alone, you three."

"Hmmm. A little sensitive are we?" Eddie suggested. He walked over and squatted beside her, taking a long, hard look at her face. "Ooo-hhh, that's right!" he exclaimed with exaggeration, pretending to have just realized what the evening held for her. "Tonight's *your* special night, too. And, if I'm not mistaken, it's date night for you, too, Tucker, my boy."

Taking advantage of the shift in attention, Shelton made a silent and hasty escape.

"Lucky guy," Ojeda grumbled, still thinking of Tucker and his date. He reached for his abandoned turkey sandwich and started to pick at it.

"Yeah, what a babe!" Cage agreed.

Casey didn't hear anyone saying anything about *her* luck. But, then, what was there to say? It was rotten, pure and simple. And she didn't particularly want to dwell on it. She was just counting the hours until it was over.

"Get a life, guys," Tucker said good-naturedly, not lifting his eyes from the daily *Bend Bulletin* spread out in front of him.

"No, I'm not kidding," Ojeda insisted. He grabbed a piece of turkey from his sandwich and crammed it in his mouth. "I'd gib anything to hab a date wid a woman like dat," he mumbled around his lunch.

"You have a date with a very nice girl, Walter," Casey snapped, stabbing at a seasoned pasta spiral with her fork. The men exchanged concerned glances. It wasn't often that they heard their team owner bark at them like that.

"Uh...sorry, Casey. You're right." Ojeda raised his eyebrows and gave the other three players a look that said, "Let's get out of here." But Cage missed it.

"What's the problem, Cas?" Eddie asked, sounding a little too compassionate. "You nervous about your date with Joe Rodeo?" Then he laughed uproariously, unable to keep a straight face any longer.

"Just forget it, Eddie," she said wearily.

"Aw, come on, Casey. I was just kidding," he said apologetically, finally noticing the lines of stress on her face.

Casey reached out and patted his shoulder. "I know, I know. I'm not mad at you...." She sighed. "I guess I'm mad at myself for getting into this mess in the first place. I don't normally go on dates with strange men. I kinda feel like I'm in over my head."

"Maybe we shouldn't have made you go up there with us, huh?" Ojeda suggested, sounding truly regretful.

"That's right. You *shouldn't* have." Tucker's words sounded like the voice of doom.

Casey blinked in surprise. She'd almost forgotten that Boyd was in the room. And he sounded more than a little upset.

"It's…all right," she said, trying to smooth things over. "I can handle it."

"What do you mean, 'handle it'?" Holmes asked.

Eddie rose from his kneeling position beside her and folded his arms across his chest. "Yeah. Are you afraid he's going to…um, want something 'extra' for his money?"

"Yeah," said Ojeda. "Guys can be like that, you know." The men were starting to sound really protective now.

Casey laid down her fork. She wasn't hungry anymore. The issue the men raised hadn't even occurred to her before. Her stomach had been in knots simply from worrying about how she was going to get through a whole evening with the yellow-toothed redneck. Now they'd really given her something to worry about.

"Oh, I'm sure I can handle it," she said breezily, sounding more confident than she felt.

"Where are you two lovebirds headed this evening?" Tucker asked, keeping his eyes glued to page two of the sports section.

"Ha, ha. Very funny, Casanova. He called on Tuesday and said he was going to make reservations at Le Bistro." At least the food would be good. Maybe they could talk about that all night.

"What time are your reservations?" he asked offhandedly.

"Uh…seven o'clock, I think. He's picking me up at six-thirty. Why?"

Tucker finally looked up from his paper and nodded comfortingly. "There will be lots of people around. You'll be fine at that hour. I wouldn't worry about a thing."

His lack of concern only annoyed her further.

"Thanks for the advice," she said coolly. "But don't worry about me. You have your own date to think about. I'm sure you'll have a wonderful time."

She was sure it was true. She only wished it were not.

It wasn't the first time Casey had agonized over what she should wear on a date. While she was far from being a clotheshorse, she knew that the right outfit could turn a guy's head and help make an impression that would last for weeks.

Which was exactly what she did *not* want to do.

She dug even further into the recesses of her closet and pulled out a fistful of hangers. From the first hung a plain black jumper and tailored white blouse, elegant in their simplicity.

Casey considered the pieces carefully. Nice. Understated. Certainly nothing flashy. But...*No, this just won't do. I don't want him to see any leg at all.*

The next two hangers held a white cabled sweater with cap sleeves and a simple, ankle-length, yellow georgette skirt. That certainly covered the leg problem.

It was close, but...*Nah. I'd still have too much shape. And speaking of shape....* Her thoughts flashed to Tucker and his blonde. *I can just imagine what she'll be wearing tonight.* She remembered Tucker's reaction to her jacquard dress on the night of the auction. She liked to think he would appreciate her in the georgette skirt. Too bad she wasn't going out on a date with *him*.

In frustration, Casey tossed the clothes on the nearby rocking chair. She needed a battle plan. The cowboy had been entirely too excited about his date with her. That's why it was important to set clear boundaries with him right from the start, beginning with her clothes. What she wanted was something that was dressy enough for the restaurant, yet still said, "Hands off."

Reaching up to the top shelf of her closet, she pulled down one of her favorite sweaters: a brushed merino wool turtleneck that hung halfway down her thighs. The deep brown color was rich and the cut chic. The only reason Casey did not wear it more often was that it was about two sizes too big.

From another hanger she retrieved a pair of loose, wool flannel trousers. Then she slipped her feet into her best stacked-heel mules and surveyed her image in the mirror.

"I look like a clown," she said to her reflection.

It was perfect.

If Casey thought that her poor fashion sense would discourage her ardent admirer, she was sadly in error. From the moment she opened her door to greet Otis Coltrain, he had worn a goofy smile on his face that would not be shaken.

As they drove to the restaurant, she tried to give him the benefit of the doubt. *All right. So he hasn't got the best dental hygiene in the world. That doesn't mean he isn't a perfectly nice guy.* Casey wasn't generally drawn to redneck types. Or ranchers. But during her brief stay in Central Oregon, she had met a number of intelligent and interesting individuals who were also cowboys and ranchers. It wasn't a culture she was familiar with, but it was one she could definitely respect.

No, it wasn't the man's profession, or even his sense of style, that bothered her. It was something more basic than that. It was his overly familiar manner. The way his smile was a little too friendly. The way he looked at her as if he wanted something...or as if he owned her.

Casey swallowed hard. In a sense, for one night, he did.

"Uh...I hope you don't mind if we don't stay out too late," she said as they jostled along in Otis's Chevy pickup. "I've got a pretty heavy-duty schedule, so I'm generally up at the crack of dawn. I'll need to be home and asleep by ten." There, she'd said it. She didn't see any point in letting the guy think she'd stay out all night with him, if that was what he had in mind.

"Not a problem," he said cheerfully. "Ah hear ya. Ah'm a workin' man mahself."

"What exactly do you do?" Casey asked.

This question launched him on a mind-numbing soliloquy about the thrills of cattle ranching. As he reeled off tale after tale revolving around details she did not have the agricultural background to understand, Casey quickly found her mind wandering.

She stared out her window at the towering Ponderosa pines and rich, red earth whizzing by. She could not help but wonder what Tucker and his blonde were discussing at that exact moment. Probably not the digestive system of cows, she decided cynically. Probably not anything to do with cows at all. Most likely, it had something to do with the woman's fascinating career—whatever that was—or how thrilled she was to be out on a date with a man who'd played in the major leagues.

Casey wondered what the blonde would think if she knew that Tucker might never make it back to the bigs. *Would he be such a prize, then? Would she still be worth her three-hundred dollar investment? Would she like him the way I do, for who he is—moody, stubborn, intense....* Casey sighed heavily. *Not to mention sweet, compassionate, and endearing.*

She, herself, hadn't quite figured out what she thought about the possibility that Tucker might move back up to the majors. He still struggled on the mound and was not nearly as consistent as he had been during his years as a major league player. And yet, he *was* getting better. It was a gradual improvement, but a steady one.

Still, she thought, he had a long way to go before Clem would consider putting him in a Stars uniform.

"Is it too hot fer ya?" Otis drawled. "Cuz ah kin open a winduh—"

"No, thanks." Casey zeroed in on his accent as a possible topic of conversation. "You're not from around here, are you?"

"No, ma'am," he admitted. "Ah'm from North Carolina."

"Really?" This, at last, captured Casey's interest. "I hear it's beautiful there."

She would have thought it impossible, but the man's grin grew a fraction wider. "Yes, *ma'am,*" he said heartily, then launched into another lengthy speech about the virtues of his hometown. By the time they reached the restaurant, Casey was mentally exhausted from trying to keep up with the one-sided conversation.

I don't know why he wanted this date, but it sure wasn't to get to know me better. He hasn't asked me a single question about myself. This fact was an irritation, but also a relief. Casey wanted nothing less than to share intimate details about her personal life with this stranger. She checked her watch. Six-fifty-five. Only a couple more hours to go.

Thankfully, the restaurant provided a bright spot to the evening. A favorite of Casey's, Le Bistro was located in a quaint old church along Third Street, Bend's main drag. In previous years, the bistro had been voted "Oregon's Best Dinnerhouse" and "One of the Twenty Best Restaurants in the Northwest." No stranger to fine dining, herself, Casey considered the light provincial cuisine to be equal, if not superior, to the four-star California restaurants she had visited with her mother and Uncle Edward over the years.

She had just settled down to study the list of entrees, however, when the interrogation began.

"So...what's a cute little thing like you doin' on a date with a ol' cowpoke like me?"

Casey laid down her menu and considered Otis Coltrain

carefully. *Good question,* she thought. With his neatly pressed, gray plaid shirt, bolo tie, and black dress jeans, he looked like something straight out of a country music video. Casey appreciated country music, but it wasn't exactly her regular style. She glanced down at her hodgepodge attire. Not that she *had* any particular style tonight.

"Ah jest mean that it seems awful strange, yer not havin' yerself a boyfriend an' all," the man said.

"Well...I'm sure stranger things have happened." Casey reached for her glass and took a long, refreshing drink of ice water.

"Ha, ha! Yer a funny thing." Otis slapped his thigh to punctuate his guffaws. "Say, what made a girl like you want to up an' buy a big ol' baseball team like the Bach'lers?"

She hesitated. It was *not* her desire to share her life story with this man. But it was also against her principles to lie. Thankfully, she was spared the need to come up with a reply when Otis Coltrain went on to answer his own question.

"Ah figger you wuz a tomboy when you wuz a kid, an' since you cain't play ball with the boys anymore, you jest decided you'd do the next best thing." He slapped the table enthusiastically. "Am ah right?"

Casey considered his assessment. There was some truth to it. "I guess it was something like that," she allowed.

He nodded knowingly. "Well, one uh these days, yer gonna wanna sell it, ah kin tell you that. There's jest no way yer gonna wanna keep runnin' around with those boys for too long. They're a rough bunch, those boys are. Most of 'em wouldn't ever think uh comin' to a nice place like this." He grinned at her. "Ah figgered a cute little thing like you would appreciate a nice place like this. You won't never see no ballplayers around here, ah jest guess!"

Casey could only stare. The man was a complete stereotype.

And a *loud* stereotype at that. All around them, people were staring. She pulled the thick collar of her turtleneck up around her ears, hoping against hope to conceal her identity.

"Oh, I think I'll be around awhile," she mumbled through the wool. "I like owning the team just fine so far, thanks," she told him. "And they really are a great group of guys. I like them a lot. I guess you're a fan, too? You must be, or you wouldn't have come to the auction."

"Well, ah jest guess ah am," Otis said. "Ah s'pose that's why ah came to see ya at the auction, there. When ah done heard that you wuz going to be auctioned off like one of my cattle, ah said to mahself, Otis, you jest git yerself down there an' you ask that little lady out on a date!"

Casey raised her menu and closed her eyes, resisting the urge to reach out and throttle him with his bolo tie. *If he calls me 'little lady' one more time....*

"It wuz a stroke of luck, really. Ah'd jest bin wonderin' how ah wuz gonna git mahself an opportunity ta meet ya—"

She sank down further in her chair. *Oh, no...here it comes....*

"—'cuz ah'd like to make you an offer you cain't refuse!"

Casey stared at him. What on earth was he implying? "And just what did you have in mind?" she said coldly.

Otis blinked at her, looking taken aback by her abruptness. "Well, ah'd have to talk to mah accountant an' all, an' look at yer books before we started negotiations—"

"What? Negotiations? Why you would think we'd have any need to negotiate is beyond me—oh!" Realization hit her. "My team? *You want to buy my team?*"

"That's right. Ah'm in the market if yer lookin' ta sell."

All at once, the absurdity of the situation struck her, and Casey collapsed in a fit of laughter.

Looking embarrassed himself, for the very first time, Otis leaned toward her across the table. "Are you all right, little lady?

If you want, ah kin get you a glass of wine or somethin'—" He scanned the room, as though looking for their waitress.

"No, no—" Casey sniffled into her napkin. "I'll be fine, really." She wiped her eyes, and black mascara came off on the white linen.

"Are ya sure ah cain't buy you a drink?" Otis drawled. "Ah don't gotta lotta sense, but ah gotta lotta money."

"Oh, no, Otis. I really don't—"

"I really can't believe we've run into you two like this," broke in a deep masculine voice from behind her.

Casey whirled at the sound and found herself staring up into the hazel eyes that haunted her dreams. A smile danced across her lips and joy filled her heart.

Tucker had come to save her.

∼ 18 ∼

I never look to the past.
RON BLOMBERG, NEW YORK YANKEES DESIGNATED HITTER, 1974

A s it turned out, Casey really didn't need saving after all. But, of course, Tucker didn't know that.

Dressed in khaki pants and a white shirt with a button-down collar, he struck Casey as an adorable, casually stylish knight in shining armor. And right now, her knight was trying to make small talk with her date.

"Well, this is just such a happy coincidence," Tucker said. Golden flecks sparkled in eyes that dared her to challenge the statement. "I think we should take advantage of our good fortune."

Casey sat up straight in her chair and scanned the dining room, but to her great relief Tucker appeared to be alone.

"I thought you had a date?"

"Oh, I do. She just stopped off at the ladies' room," he explained.

While Casey was processing this disappointing bit of information, Boyd flagged down a waitress and convinced her to move Casey and Otis to a table for four by the window. Casey hated to stand up. In her frumpy outfit, she wanted nothing more than to sink beneath the table. However, since Tucker was determined, staying put was not an option. She and Otis were just settling in at their new table when Tucker's date appeared.

Casey drew a deep breath. The woman looked every bit as ravishing as she had the night of the auction. This time, she was dressed in tapered houndstooth check slacks with a cerulean linen blouse that brought out the violet in her eyes...and fit snugly in all the right places. A wide black head-band held back her long golden hair, and she wore an expensive-looking gold choker at her throat.

Like a turtle retreating into its shell, Casey instinctively retracted her neck even further into her oversized sweater.

Tucker did not seem to notice her discomfort, however, as he began making the introductions. "Eleanor, this is Casey Foster, and..."

"Otis Coltrain, ma'am!" Casey's date supplied heartily.

"Yes. Otis Coltrain." Tucker twisted his lips, as if the words tasted bitter. "Otis, Casey...this is Eleanor Bishop."

The woman stepped close to Tucker's side and placed one hand on his arm in a familiar gesture. "It's a pleasure," she said graciously to Casey and Otis, giving each a courteous nod. Then she turned her full attention back to Boyd. "Tucker, don't you think we should be finding our table?"

"Actually, Eleanor, I thought we'd join Casey and Otis," he suggested. When she opened her mouth to protest, he lowered his lips close to her ear and whispered something.

Unable to bear seeing the two of them so close, Casey tipped her face downward and pretended to be scraping imaginary crumbs from the linen tablecloth.

"Well...I suppose it wouldn't hurt to eat together, since we're already here," Eleanor said, but there was a little pout in her voice.

"Good! I knew you'd be pleased." Tucker appeared relieved to have the matter settled. Following the boy-girl seating arrangement, he pulled out the empty chair beside Otis and offered it to his date.

"I hope this is good timing?" he asked the other man, while seating himself a moment later. "I didn't interrupt anything important, I trust?" He reached for a crystal goblet and raised the glass of water to his lips.

Otis warmed to the topic. "Actually, ya did walk in jest as ah wuz making Casey here a proposition."

As Tucker sputtered, tiny droplets of water sprayed across the table in front of him.

"This little lady's one tough cookie, though, ah tell you," Otis continued, undaunted. "Turned me down flat, an' ah'm not used ta bein' turned down."

Looking somewhat relieved, Tucker wiped the table in front of him with his linen napkin.

"That's all right, though," Otis continued. "'Cuz Otis Coltrain ain't a man who takes no fer an answer! Ah know what ah want. Ah know how to fight fer it. An' ah aim to keep trying 'til the little lady gives me what ah'm after!"

Casey stared at her silverware, trying not to laugh. It was clear from his expression what Tucker thought Otis meant by a "proposition."

With a look of horror on his face, Tucker leaned toward Casey and whispered, "For heaven's sake, Casey! This guy sounds like a total *lech*. Do you want me to get you out of here?"

The offer could not have pleased Casey more. At that moment, she wanted nothing so much as an excuse—*any* excuse—to steal Tucker away from the beauty seated on the other side of him. *We can just say that I have a headache. Or that we've got to call an emergency baseball practice... No, Casey. That's absurd. No one would fall for such a ridiculous story!*

Casey was terrible at telling fibs, perhaps because it was a practice she did not condone. Thankfully, her inability to form a reasonable excuse gave her just enough time to reconsider.

No, lying would be unacceptable. There was no reason for it anyway. Otis was after her team...not her body. And whatever the sultry Eleanor was after...well, that was none of Casey's business. Like it or not, she was responsible for bringing the pitcher and the blonde bombshell together. She couldn't undo it now. Whatever happened next was between Tucker and Eleanor and God.

Besides, she had to be honest with Tucker. He meant too much to her to risk driving a wedge between them. Surely, one day the truth would come out that she hadn't been in the kind of danger that he feared, and then she would have to explain why she had dragged him away from his date under false pretenses.

"It's really not what you're thinking," she explained in subdued tones. "Otis isn't such a bad guy, once you get to know him."

Tucker pulled back a fraction of an inch and gave her a hard stare. "I can't believe you're actually going to 'get to know him.'"

"Boyd!" She narrowed her eyes at him. "You take that back!"

"Take what back?"

"I don't know! Whatever you're implying. It sounded bad."

He glanced at the thick-necked cowboy who was, by this time, conversing animatedly with Tucker's date. "Well, I guess I can't really see you going for this guy. I'm sorry." He studied Casey's face closely. "But...what if it was some other guy?" he whispered.

She shifted uncomfortably under his scrutiny. "I'm not really sure what you're asking. If you're wondering if I would 'get to know' some man intimately on a physical level, outside of marriage, I can assure you that the answer is no."

Restlessly, she reached for her napkin and began to fold it

into tiny squares. "Now, if you're asking me if I'm open to 'getting to know' a man on a romantic level...well, that's different. I'm not looking to get a boyfriend just for the sake of having one. But I certainly pray that God will send someone wonderful into my life someday. But for now, I'm happy. I'm enjoying life as it comes. And I'm prepared to wait for a man who loves God as much as I do...a man who will love me deeply, and who I can love through good times and hardships, because I know life will bring both." Her voice was still low, but held a note of finality.

Tucker gave Casey a thoughtful look. Then, without another word, he leaned back in his chair and picked up his menu. Soon, the table conversation was spinning back in the direction of cows and investment portfolios, since Eleanor was a stockbroker and was involved in local cattle dealings. But as the evening wore on, Tucker continued to steal furtive glances in Casey's direction, an act that reassured her that their conversation was never far from his mind.

Two hours later, Casey's date had, indeed, ended, although the conclusion came in a very different manner than she'd anticipated.

Throughout dinner, Eleanor and Otis continued to exchange investment advice, and before long, as it became apparent that Otis was a much more lucrative target than Tucker, Eleanor's entire focus of interest shifted. The two swapped stories, business strategies, and eventually phone numbers. Finally, citing a report that she thought might be helpful to Otis, Eleanor mentioned that it would be convenient to pick it up at her office that evening and suggested that the rancher drive her home.

By nine o'clock, Casey and Tucker were alone.

It didn't take much wheedling for him to convince her that they should take a late-night stroll, and Casey soon found herself walking beside him down by Mirror Pond at Drake Park.

"You know, we really couldn't have planned that better if we'd tried," Tucker said brightly.

"Oh, really?" Casey inhaled deeply, enjoying the cool, fresh evening air. "I rather thought you liked Eleanor."

"Now, Casey..." He smiled. "She's not my type, and you know it."

"Hmmm. You could have fooled me. I saw you whispering in her ear before dinner."

"Ye-es." Tucker's smile grew to a Cheshire-cat grin.

"Well, are you going to tell me what you two were so cozy about?" she asked impatiently.

He remained silent for a moment—holding back, teasing her—before explaining. "I simply suggested that Mr. Coltrain might be an excellent client. She's very business-minded, as you know by now. I figured the two of them might hit it off. And they did...which suits me just fine. Because I can assure you," he said warmly, "I am definitely *not* feeling very business-minded." Casey felt her cheeks flush with pleasure. "And don't pretend you didn't want to get rid of them as much as I did," he scolded.

"I don't know what you're talking about!"

"Oh, you don't?" Tucker adopted an exaggerated swagger and broke into a perfect imitation of Otis Coltrain. "Well, then, little lady, ah'll jest have to remind ya—"

Casey smirked. "All right! You win. But really, you have to admit, Otis wasn't all that bad once you got to know him."

"Humph. Well, I'll admit I felt a lot better once I realized that he hadn't actually propositioned you." During the appetizers, Casey had finally broken down and explained what she and Otis had been discussing before Tucker and Eleanor arrived.

"Just so you know…I could have let him be your new boss," she said warningly.

"Ooh. Now *there's* an ugly prospect." He shuddered, then asked casually, "What about it, Casey? Do you think you'll ever sell the Bachelors?"

"Well, I know I never want to auction them again!" Tucker gratified her with a warm laugh.

As they walked, Casey watched the toes of her rounded black shoes peek out from beneath her brown trouser legs. "Seriously, though…I'm not sure," she said, lengthening her step to match his. "Maybe someday, I guess. But right now, I really believe this is the best place for me to be…the place where God wants me. The only regret I have is that I never got very far in my sportscasting career." She shrugged. "It's not that I'm so driven by success. It's just that I *do* like to do my best at whatever I tackle." She considered for a moment. "So I might want to take another stab at sportscasting one of these days. It still bothers me that I spent so much of my time challenging people. I didn't make a lot of friends that way."

"It's hard for me to believe that," Tucker admitted.

"You've got to be joking!"

He chuckled—a warm, hearty sound that made Casey's insides ache. "No, I've got a pretty good picture in my head of what it means to get you riled up. It's just that you're so…kind to everybody. I can't really see you making enemies in the business."

"Oh, I don't have enemies, exactly," Casey admitted. "It's not like I chewed out every major sports figure I met, or anything like that. It's just that—well, take Otis, for example. He's a little odd, but basically a good guy, right? Yet he's convinced that a woman like me—or any woman, for that matter—could never fit in with a bunch of ballplayers. Assumptions like that used to drive me crazy, and I'd lose my cool."

"You didn't lose your cool with Otis tonight," Tucker pointed out.

"No. That's true," she said. "Although I came pretty close."

"And you haven't lost your cool with me. At least, not for a while."

Casey thought about that. "This experience has been good for me. I started out with the team under the assumption that I had to hold my tongue. I wanted to be a leader Uncle Edward would have been proud of. And I didn't want to give anyone a reason to say, 'Hey, there's that team with the emotional woman in charge.' I figured I had a lot to prove.

"At first, I was really frustrated," she admitted. "With you, Hatch, Gibby, Shelton...even Gordy acted more like a father figure to me than a peer."

"You have good relationships with all of those people now—except for Hatch, of course, but he's gone anyway."

Casey stopped and turned to him. "I know!" she said animatedly. "It was the strangest thing. I was going along, struggling. Then, somewhere along the way, I just learned that I was able to help my cause a lot more by being responsible and trustworthy—and by *earning* respect instead of just waiting for people to give it to me.

"I still get frustrated at having to prove myself in situations where men might not have to. But as time goes on, I'm handling it better. And I'm seeing more of the good in those same people who used to drive me up the wall."

Casey turned back toward the path, and they resumed walking. "What about you, Tucker?" She tried to make her voice sound casual. "Think you'll be sticking with the Bachelors for a while?"

"I'd say you probably know that better than I do." He spoke matter-of-factly, seemingly without resentment. "What's the word from Phoenix?"

"Oh, it's not really something we discuss…" Casey hedged.

Tucker stopped and pulled her to a halt, grasping her fingers in his. "It's okay," he said gently. His eyes begged for the truth. "I can handle it."

"Well—" It was hard to think with him holding her hands like that. "I haven't really talked with Clem in several weeks," she said finally. "Not about you, anyway. But the last time we spoke, he, uh…well, he wasn't exactly thrilled with your performance."

Tucker nodded. "I can imagine that he wouldn't be."

"Of course, that was awhile ago," she said more cheerfully, hating to see the look of grim resignation on his face. "You've been doing much better in the past weeks."

"Thanks. That's sweet of you." Tucker squeezed her fingers. "But I've been thinking a lot lately, and I've been wondering if maybe it's time for me to accept the fact that I'm not good enough for the bigs anymore. Maybe I need to retire to the bush leagues."

Casey tried to read his blank expression. "Would that be so bad?"

"No. Actually, it wouldn't." He sounded almost surprised to hear the words as they tumbled out of his mouth. "I can make this work, if I have to. I'm finding that playing in the minors is a perfectly respectable career. I have to admit, this league is starting to grow on me." His fingers left her hands and began to trace lightly over the skin of her forearms, just under her loose-fitting sleeves. "And so are you."

"I am?" Casey's heart skipped a beat.

"Yes, Casey. You are." His smile was tender. "Did you know that I thought I had things all figured out until you came along? I was going to get my pitching back on track, move up to the Stars, and become a big fat success.

"And then—" Tucker withdrew one hand from her arm and

raised it to gently stroke the slope of her cheek. "Then I met a wonderful woman who reminded me about the things that really matter in life: loving people and serving God."

Casey held her breath.

"For the past two months, I've been working on the serving God part. I've been talking to him every day. I'm starting to wear out that Bible you gave me!" He laughed. "I haven't talked with you about this before because I wanted to do it without your help. It's not that I didn't trust you. I just didn't want to use you as a crutch."

Hearing those words, Casey almost wondered if he had somehow been reading her thoughts.

"That's normal, Tucker," she reassured him. "I know it is. I feel so silly now...because I actually did wonder if you might read your Bible or come to church because you wanted to please me."

"That's not silly. I'd call it a valid concern. That's what happened to me in college, although there wasn't a girl involved."

"I know it's valid," Casey told him. "But I also know that you have a very good heart and you truly want to serve God. I didn't give you enough credit. This time, I was the one making assumptions about someone. I'm sorry. Falling away from God is a pretty common experience for believers. The important thing is that you've turned back to him again."

"I'm glad you understand." Tucker reached out and folded her into his warm embrace. "It was important to me to do this right. I failed at it once before. I made a commitment to God, and I fell away—" He stopped abruptly and gave Casey a funny look.

"There I go again! Listen to me...I'm still talking about this in terms of failure and victory." He shook his head ruefully. "I guess old habits die hard. I'm working on it, though. I don't want my life to be a constant battle to 'win.' I'm tired of turning myself into a pretzel emotionally, as though I'm still trying to please my dad. From now on, the only ones I'm going to worry about pleasing are God and myself," he said emphatically.

He gripped Casey by the elbows, held her out at arm's length, and bestowed upon her the most loving look she had ever been given. "And you, if you'll have me," he said.

Casey laid one hand against the softness of Tucker's shirt, feeling the strong, steady beat of his heart beneath her fingers. "Nothing would please me more," she said with a tender smile.

Then she lifted her face for the gentle kiss that was to come.

~ *19* ~

*Sitting on the bench watching him pitch, I often forgot
I was a ballplayer. I became a fan.*

RUBE MILLER, NEW YORK GIANTS PITCHER,
ON TEAMMATE CHRISTY MATHEWSON

FRIDAY, AUGUST 8

Martin Ruger swaggered up to the plate to lead off the Pioneer fourth. Apparently anticipating a repeat of the crushing victory his team had scored on the Bachelors' opening day, he grinned from ear to ear, exuding confidence and pride.

Tucker met Ruger's eyes as he had almost three months before. The challenge was still there.

Refusing to acknowledge the unspoken dare, he drew a deep breath and took a moment to focus. *Remember why you're here, Tucker. Give it your best. Play with your heart.*

Nodding at the catcher's signal, he started off with a fastball high. Ruger took the bait and swung.

"Steeee-rike one!" cried the ump.

The batter spat on the ground. Once again, he tried to shake Boyd's confidence, this time with an angry glare. By now, however, Tucker was in his own world, where nothing existed but the sun at his back, the breeze on his face, the comfortable weight of the ball in his hand…and peace in his heart.

He nodded at Ojeda's signal, wound up a second time, and let loose with a backdoor slider.

Throwing all his weight into it, the Pioneers' lead-off man took the swing as the ball flew in on the outside corner.

"Steeee-rike two!" cried the ump.

Ruger swore and threw the bat down in disgust. Tucker ignored him. There was no way he was going to get drawn into the man's anger and frustration. He wasn't playing those games. Not anymore.

It had been a long journey to the place he was today. After years of "going through the motions" as a professional baseball player, he was enjoying the game—and enjoying life—as never before. For the first time in his career, perhaps for the first time ever, passion partnered with skill, and the results were tangible, both on and off the field.

In the past months he had gone from being an unpredictable, inconsistent major league has-been to a solid pitcher with respectable stats and nerves of steel. While he once had been ruled by feelings of inadequacy that undermined his performance, today he was confident, self-assured…and a force for the Bachelors' competition to contend with.

His tantrum over, Ruger finally resumed his position at bat.

Ojeda called the pitch. Four fingers. Time for the change-up.

Behind the shield of his glove, Tucker positioned his fingers on the ball in a V-shaped, split-finger grip, then wound up and threw the ball directly at Ojeda.

Ruger swung…and missed.

"Steeee-rike three! You're out!"

Finally, Tucker grinned. But his smile of satisfaction was directed not at his rival, who was now storming off the field in a childish fit of rage, but at the woman he knew would share in his happiness.

He was not disappointed. From behind the dugout's Cyclone fence, Casey threw him a radiant smile, and Tucker felt an overwhelming surge of emotion. He was, at that moment, the happiest he had ever been.

Four weeks had passed since he and Casey had shared their first kiss by Mirror Pond. To Tucker, that day marked the beginning of a whole new life for him—a life of hope and beauty, intimacy and connection. Every day he thanked God for bringing Casey into his life, and for drawing *him* back into a spiritual relationship that made their romance—indeed, made all things—possible.

Each day was a new adventure. He never knew what Casey would be up to next. Just the previous Saturday, a simple shared chore had turned into a hilarious mock battle.

"What in heaven's name do you *do* to this thing to get it so filthy?" Tucker had said, holding his dripping sponge aloft over the dirt-covered, late-model Ford Bronco that was Casey's pride and joy. With plenty of storage room for her baseball equipment, skis, and other athletic paraphernalia, Casey considered it the perfect sportswoman's vehicle, and she had told him she wanted it to "shine."

"I *use* it," she said haughtily, sounding wounded. "The way God intended."

"Now, Casey," Tucker admonished her. "Even *I* know God didn't create Broncos."

"All right," she allowed. "Then I'm using it the way *Ford* intended."

Still looking offended, she glanced around for a weapon, then grabbed a sudsy red rag from the bucket at her feet and heaved it at him. Delighted, she watched as the cloth spun through the air in a perfect windmill pattern, flinging shiny little droplets in a spiral, before hitting Tucker squarely on the forehead.

"Oof!" He fell backward and caught the cloth as it fell. Reaching up with his other hand, he wiped the dirty, soapy water from his face. "Hey! What's this? All right, missy. You asked for it!"

Casey squealed happily as he charged around the Bronco after her. She ran for her best weapon of defense: the garden hose.

"What are you—?" He recoiled in mock horror. "Now... don't do anything you're gonna regret."

"Ha!" She threw back her head and laughed. "I have no regrets! I am Casey Foster, Queen of the Bachelors!" She raised a graceful arm and pointed at him dramatically. "You, Pitcher Boyd, are at my command!"

Tucker stopped in his tracks and set his hands squarely on his hips. "Like fun, I'm at your command!" he scoffed.

Rising to his challenge, Casey gripped the nozzle in her hand and, with a shout of triumph, blasted him full-force with a wide, icy stream.

"Stop! Sto-*oooop,* I said!" His cries for help had done no good. She was merciless.

But he *had* gotten his revenge. Tucker remembered with satisfaction the bucket of water he had subsequently dumped over Casey's head.

The water fight had left them both soaked and exhausted. Afterward, Casey had volunteered to fix his mussed, towel-dried hair with her electric blow-dryer. "Don't want my star pitcher catching a cold!" she'd proclaimed. He still could feel the gentle touch of her hands as she ran them through his hair, teasing each damp strand into submission under her expert fingers.

Tucker shook his head, trying to clear it. The next batter was up. Ojeda was waiting. Daydreaming about Casey would have to wait.

But not for long.

Casey watched, spellbound, as Tucker struck out another batter. She'd witnessed countless incredible plays executed by hundreds of great players over the years, but "Big Time" Boyd surpassed them all. As an athlete—and as a man, she thought—Tucker brought new meaning to the phrase "poetry in motion."

"Ya got a call, Casey," Gibby said, jerking his head in the direction of the phone mounted at the end of the dugout. Then his eyes traced her line of vision, and he smirked. "By the way, ya might wanna wipe that goofy grin off your face."

Casey knew that she should listen to his advice. Surely everyone could see by now how thoroughly smitten she was with the man on the pitcher's mound.

But she didn't care.

"Maybe I *can't* stop smiling," she said lightly.

Gibby rolled his eyes. "I dunno," he said seriously. "Sounds like love to me."

Casey ignored his teasing comment and went to retrieve the phone. It was good to still have the kid around. Gibson had been scheduled to move on to Phoenix as early as six weeks into the season, but a strained muscle had kept him from playing for over two weeks. Besides, she didn't mind his teasing; she knew he was happy for her. In fact, the entire team had been amused, but genuinely thrilled, when they'd found out she and Boyd had started dating.

It still felt like a miracle. The relationship she had wanted most—and had been most afraid she would never have—was actually hers. But she did not take anything for granted. Each day was one to be treasured. Casey's heart overflowed with adoration for the man she was coming to respect and admire more and more each day.

Gibby's dig had not been without a point, though. From the

beginning, the guys had teased Casey and Tucker about being "in looo-ove." When they had kept the details of their relationship private, the players were a bit disappointed. If they had to watch their owner and lead pitcher "mooning" about each other, they said, they wanted to be in on all the juicy details.

As far as private expressions of their feelings went, Casey had not yet told Tucker that she loved him—nor had he made such a declaration to her. Both wanted to take things slowly, carefully. Yet what she had not confessed with her lips, she already knew in her heart to be fact.

She was in love. Crazily, overwhelmingly, head over heels in love. Casey Foster had never had so much to cherish.

Or so much to lose, she thought, as she lifted the receiver to her ear.

"Casey!" Al Clement's voice crackled over the wire, and Casey's heart fell. Clem could be calling for any number of reasons, but the one most likely was the one she feared. "How are ya?" There was an edge to his voice. Casey knew that tone. He wanted something.

"I'm fine, Clem," she said warily. She sat heavily on the dugout bench and gripped the phone hard. "What's up?" But she knew in her heart what was coming. A feeling of dread consumed her.

"Just wanted to get the latest update on your ace pitchers," the Stars' manager informed her. "You promised to keep me posted, you know, and I haven't heard a peep out of you in weeks," he accused.

A wave of guilt washed over Casey. She'd known all along that she should call Clem and tell him about Tucker's improvement, but somehow she'd always managed to find an excuse to put it off. Now, confronted with the very situation she'd dreaded, she realized that her actions hadn't helped Tucker, the Stars, ...or herself.

"Sorry about that, Clem. I've been pretty busy," she told him. "Winning games, you know," she said brightly. *And falling in love....*

For one insane moment, she considered withholding the truth about Tucker's improvement. But she quickly dismissed the idea. No matter what she felt in her heart, she could not rely upon lies to prolong their relationship. Still, she wouldn't make it easy for Clem. She wasn't about to volunteer any information.

"So...?"

"What do you want to know?" She could picture Clem in her mind, leaning back in his expensive gray office chair, with his arms folded behind his smooth, round head.

"How's Gibby's arm?"

"Wish I had better news to offer," she said. "He's still healing."

The man grunted, then asked the question she feared most. "How about Boyd? What's his record these days? Didn't you say he was starting to pitch better?"

Casey took a deep breath. "Fourteen and eight," she told him.

Clem let out a long, low whistle. "Not bad. That's *quite* an improvement, I'd say. Wasn't he six and six the last time we talked?"

"Something like that," Casey said noncommittally.

Clem fell silent. For a moment, only static crackled over the wire. "What's the matter, kiddo?" he finally asked. "You sound like something's wrong."

"I'm fine, Clem." Casey focused her eyes on her cross-trainers, planted firmly against the rich red earth. Placing one hand over the mouthpiece, she took a quick, deep breath, trying not to cry. There was no point in telling him about the personal crisis his phone call had triggered. Her situation wouldn't change the fact that Clem had a right—even a responsibility—to offer Tucker an invitation to the majors if that was best for the team…and for Tucker's career. Besides, she wasn't yet ready to tell Clem that she had fallen in love with one of her players.

"Casey," Clem pushed. "Come on. I know I'm not Edward, but I care about you like you were my own niece. You can tell me what's going on."

The man's concern was only slightly comforting. "I guess I'm just not all that thrilled about losing Tucker," she said. "I'm…getting kind of attached to him."

"Is that all?" He sounded relieved. "Well, of course you're not thrilled! Who'd want to lose a pitcher who's fourteen and eight? But don't worry now. You haven't lost him yet, and you may not after all. I've still got a full roster, although we've had a few injuries. I need to see how Lopez's arm looks in a few days. But don't worry, kid. We're all a part of one big family. You can keep in touch with Boyd if you want, and hopefully you'll get to see him playing in the Series!" he predicted confidently.

"I think that's great, Clem," Casey lied, trying to sound enthusiastic. "It looks like we might be headed to the division play-offs ourselves." *Thanks to Tucker. Too bad he might not get to stick around to see it happen.…*

"Well, that's just great, kiddo! Your uncle would be proud."

After several more probing questions, Clem had gotten all the information he needed. Telling Casey that he would be in touch, he wished her good luck on the game and hung up, leaving the dead receiver dangling in her hand and a battle of emotions warring in her heart.

What's the matter with you, Casey? You think you love him? Well, then…be happy for him! An opportunity like this comes once in a lifetime for most guys. He's been to the show once, and now he may actually be able to go back—just like he has wanted to do all season. It's a miracle that he has improved so much. God has healed him, so be grateful, you selfish girl.

"I guess that was Clements?"

Casey raised her head at the sound of Gordy's voice. "You heard?" she said glumly.

The coach nodded and drew her toward the far end of the dugout, away from the other players. Casey sat forlornly, and Gordy settled his ample body onto the bench next to her. The two sat in silence for several minutes, staring out at the action on the field.

"You know, Tucker's come a long way," Olson said after a while. "I have to admit, at the beginning of the season, none of us thought he'd be worth much." A toothpick hung from his lips as he shifted the sliver of wood from one side of his mouth to the other.

"The thing is, we couldn't figure out what was wrong. Shelton worked him a lot, but aside from a few minor glitches, it wasn't really Boyd's form that was the problem." Gordy leaned forward in his seat, with his hands against his knees. "If something hadn't changed, though, he'd have been given a one-way ticket back to Wisconsin."

Keeping her eyes trained on the ground, Casey listened to the soft cadence of the man's rumbling voice, trying to draw comfort from the sound.

"In fact, he should have been on that plane back in *February*," Gordon said. He gave the word added emphasis, as if it had some special meaning.

With one toe, she played with a small stone beneath her feet. "I don't know what you're talking about."

Gordon wasn't buying it. "Yeah, you do, Casey. Clem told me that you convinced him to keep Boyd on, even after he stunk up spring training."

"What do you mean, 'convinced' him? I told Clem that I wanted Boyd for the good of the team." She paused under

Gordy's knowing look. "What? So he wasn't so hot at camp. That doesn't change the fact that he's an incredible talent with years of major league experience."

Gordon shook his head. "Casey, Boyd was playing rotten, and you know it."

"Maybe I was just willing to take a chance," she suggested.

"Maybe you just have a good heart."

She sighed. "Gordy, please. I know you're trying to help, but…"

He finally relented. "All right, I'll say my piece, then leave you alone." He continued to gnaw at the toothpick. "You're going to be okay, kid. Remember that. You have a lot to feel good about, you know. Tucker really cares about you. You've turned his life around. He's playing up to his potential today because you saw something in him that the rest of us didn't. You reached out to him, and you made a difference."

Casey heard his words, but she could only feel pain. "I just feel so dumb! I haven't even lost him yet, and already it hurts so much! I should have known better than to get involved with a ballplayer." She wanted to hit a wall, rip a towel in two. "You know, my dad left my mom when I was a kid because he wanted to play ball," she admitted.

If he was surprised, Gordy did not show it. "Did he succeed?"

"I haven't ever heard his name, so I guess not."

He nodded. "That stinks. It must have hurt a lot. But you're not a kid anymore, and Tucker's not your dad. You'll be okay. You just wait and see. God's got a plan for you two."

"I don't know, Gordy," she said cynically. "I don't really think of him as the great big Yenta in the sky."

"Well, now, I don't know about that," he said. "Maybe he isn't the Cosmic Matchmaker. But I don't think the people we love drop into our lives by accident. And I'm sure that God

189

cares deeply about what's going on in our lives. No matter what happens, it'll all work out for the best."

"I just can't believe I got myself into this situation!" Casey said. "It's crazy."

Gordy pitched his gummed-up toothpick onto the ground. "In principle, I'd agree with you. It doesn't seem like it's such a good idea for the owner of a team to date a player." He laughed. "Not that the situation comes up that often!"

Casey didn't even crack a smile.

"Okay," he said, growing more serious. "Obviously, all kinds of complications can occur…and now one has. But the truth of the matter is, you two are really good for each other. And things just might work out better than you think."

"Do me a favor, Gordy?" Casey pleaded as he stood up to go. "Don't say anything about Clem's phone call to anyone? I want to handle this myself."

"Sure thing," he told her, then patted her shoulder and followed through on his promise to leave her alone with her thoughts.

She didn't have long to compose herself. The inning ended, and the players jogged in from the field, with Tucker at the head of the pack. She watched as he spotted her and headed her way.

She felt unprepared to face him. What would she say? How and when should she break the news to him?

"How's the most beautiful team owner in the world?" Tucker asked, as he came over to stand beside her and watched the Pioneers' pitcher take the mound.

"Great!" she said cheerfully. She, too, faced the field, thankful for the excuse not to meet his eyes. She couldn't tell him. Not yet. Not here. Not unless she wanted to fall apart in front of nearly three thousand people.

"It feels good out there today," he said with satisfaction. "I feel like I'm finally starting to catch my rhythm."

Casey felt the muscles in her stomach tighten. "You're playing beautifully, Tucker." She packed the words with as much enthusiasm as she could muster, but the compliment still fell flat.

"Hey, Case?" Picking up on her tone, Tucker stepped in front of her and looked down into her face. "What's wrong, sweetie?"

She shrugged and avoided his eyes, looking around him toward the field. "Nothing."

Wrinkles of worry creased Tucker's forehead. "It isn't nothing," he said.

She groaned inwardly. *Great. You managed to hide your feelings from him for what...a whole fifteen seconds?*

"Well, actually—" Casey stopped. She couldn't go through with it. Finally, she raised her eyes to his. "Actually, I'm not really feeling all that well. Would you mind terribly if I begged off of dinner tonight? I feel like I just need time to rest." *And to think.*

Tucker eyed her uncertainly. It was clear that her mood shift concerned him. "What's the matter? Is it your stomach? Do you think it's something you ate?"

"I don't know—"

"Because I can take you home and make you some chicken noodle soup. Tucker Nightingale, you know." He smiled.

"Tucker—"

"It's no trouble," he assured her gently. "I *like* taking care of you."

"Tucker!" Frustration caused her to nearly shout. "This isn't something you can fix. I just need to go home early. Okay?"

"Okay," he said doubtfully. Then, seeing the anxious look on her face, he folded her into a gentle hug. "Sorry. My protective instincts just kicked in. Of course you can take some time to rest tonight, if that's what you need." He looked at her tenderly. "Promise you'll call if you need me?"

Casey nodded against the comfort of his broad chest. But as her cheek brushed against the rough fabric of his uniform, she realized that the days they shared were numbered.

Pretty soon, phone calls to Tucker would be all she had left.

~ 20 ~

If the world was perfect, it wouldn't be.
YOGI BERRA, HALL OF FAME CATCHER

SATURDAY, AUGUST 9

Casey tossed the toasted bagel back onto her plate, sending a tiny drop of jam flying. Sleep had eluded her the entire night. What had made her think she'd be able to eat?

Usually, Saturday mornings were Casey's favorite time of the week. Since the beginning of the summer, her regular routine had been to sleep in until nine, rise just long enough to flip on her coffeemaker, then laze about in bed while the smell of French roast filled the house. When she got the urge to eat, she toasted a bagel, or grabbed a baguette, and carried it out to the deck to enjoy her simple meal beneath the towering Ponderosa pines. As she ate her breakfast and sipped her coffee, she flipped through the morning paper, or simply enjoyed the rush of wind in the trees, while filling her lungs with the cleansing mountain air.

After breakfast, she'd run a hot bath, wrap her hair in a bath-towel turban, and immerse herself up to the neck in fragrant bubbles. As the heat of the water eased her aching muscles, she made a conscious effort to erase all worries and stresses from her mind. Only when the water had turned uncomfortably cool would she emerge, relaxed and ready for the tasks she had planned for the day.

This morning, however, she could not bring herself to even begin the comforting ritual. She had started her day with a cool, bracing shower, and even her favorite coffee tasted bitter to her tongue. There was no point in trying to relax. She'd tossed and turned all night and had still found no peace of mind. The last thing she wanted was more time to reflect. What she needed was a project. Something to occupy her mind and divert her attention from her present troubles. Something positive.

Much of her time and energy over the past few months had been spent planning the team promotions that had been so popular with the local fans. To her surprise, she had found these activities challenging and rewarding, even though she sometimes felt like a cruise director. Now, only one event remained: the much-publicized Bachelor Party.

Although the team could be headed for the division playoffs, Casey had scheduled this event as a special thank-you to the fans to be celebrated at the end of the regular season. This event, too, had been planned well in advance, and the details triple checked. But, Casey told herself, she could head down to her office and go over the details one more time. It was certainly better than moping around the house all morning, and she liked the idea of having work to do, as an excuse not to see Tucker.

The night before, he'd called, but Casey had let her machine pick it up. "Hi, it's me," he'd said unnecessarily. "You're not answering, so I guess you're asleep already. I just wanted to let you know that I'm thinking about you. I'll say a little prayer tonight, for you to feel better. Good-night, sweetie." Then he'd clicked off, leaving her feeling more wretched than before.

Casey threw on an oversized white T-shirt and a pair of faded navy drawstring shorts, slipped her feet into her favorite pair of Adidas, and took off for the ballpark.

Casey sat at her desk, staring blankly at the Bachelor Party plans and delivery confirmations before her. The phone had already rung several times, but she stubbornly refused to answer it. *I have every right to want to work undisturbed,* she told herself, despite the fact that the stack of papers on her desk remained virtually untouched.

She tried to push away her feelings of guilt. She had no reason to believe that it was Tucker calling. It could just as easily be a fan, calling to see if there was a recorded schedule of events. Yet she was sure it was him.

Even if it was Tucker, he wouldn't necessarily think that I'm ignoring him, she tried to reassure herself. *He'd probably just assume that if I'm not home and not at work, then I must be feeling better and have gone out to run errands. Wouldn't he?*

It wasn't that she didn't want to see him. In fact, she ached for the warm comfort of his embrace. But she simply did not know what she would say to him when she saw him face-to-face. Or, perhaps more truthfully, she dreaded what she would have to say when she saw him face-to-face. Once she broke the news that Clem was interested in him for the Stars, Tucker would be thrilled—as she should be. And from that point on, it would be impossible to forget, even for a moment, that their time together was only temporary.

Casey wondered briefly if that was the only feasible outcome. Surely in this day and age it was possible to conduct a successful long-distance relationship? But she knew this could only be a short-term solution. Maybe she *should* consider accepting Otis Coltrain's offer to buy the team. She'd taken on the challenge because she'd known that was her uncle's desire...and she loved it. But that didn't necessarily mean that she planned on remaining an owner forever. Still, even if she did sell, what would she do then? Follow Tucker around the country? That was hardly appropriate, especially since the man hadn't even told her that he loved her.

The only other option she could see was to ask Tucker to give up his shot at the big leagues, and that was something she just could not do. Baseball was in his blood, as it was in hers. He'd waited too long, and worked too hard, to walk away from it now.

That's it, Casey—isn't it? You're afraid you'll find out that Tucker loves baseball more than he could ever love you. Just like Dad.

Tucker wasn't her father, Gordy had said. But still...

She agonized over the situation for what seemed like days. There was no answer—only more questions. When to tell him? What to say? How to let go of the one thing she wanted most in the world....

Feeling the sudden need to throw something—and *hard*—Casey grabbed her Louisville mitt off the top of her file cabinet, stopped off at the equipment room for a bag of balls, and stormed out to the field.

As she stepped up to the mound, her thoughts drifted back to the day Tucker had caught her in midpitch. *"Hey, Foster! You're rotating too soon."* She smiled at the memory of how he'd playfully turned her unsolicited coaching advice back on her.

Instinctively, she turned to scan the field, as if she might find him standing behind her, smirking. To her relief—and dismay—he wasn't there. The solitude was unsettling.

Late in the afternoon, the park would be opened for the evening's game. But for now, the stadium was hauntingly empty. Yet everywhere she looked, she saw visions of Tucker: pitching, helping a teammate perfect his curveball, encouraging the rookies with his experience and leadership. Yes, he was ready to go back to the big leagues.

Shaking off the memories, unable to face the thought of life without Tucker, Casey reached down into the bag and pulled out the first ball. For several minutes, she held it in her hand, until the inanimate object seemed to take on human characteristics. What had once been a friend now felt like an enemy, and Casey flung it hard over home plate, suddenly hating the ball and everything it represented.

Feeling a tiny rush of adrenaline, she grabbed a second ball. This time she did not hesitate, but immediately hurled the object straight toward an imaginary catcher, feeling a sense of satisfaction at the loud crash it made as it hit the wire mesh fence.

With no regard for form, she continued to fire sloppy pitches from the mound until the bag was nearly empty and her breath uneven. Running on less than full steam after her sleepless night, she felt suddenly and completely drained. With one last, weak toss of the ball, Casey fell to her knees, and the emotions she'd held in check finally broke through in the form of a few small tears.

It was unbelievable that once again she was losing the man she loved most in the world. During her childhood, baseball had seemed like an ally, occasionally bringing her wayward dad back into her life. During her college years, it had sometimes seemed like the enemy responsible for stealing him away.

As a fledgling sportscaster, she'd had to face those mixed feelings, and during the past two years, the game had seemed like an ally once more—giving her opportunities to draw even closer to her beloved uncle. Then it had brought Tucker into her life, a man she believed she could love forever. Yet now, baseball had turned on her once again, and she felt an impending sense of doom.

You're being ridiculous, Casey, she told herself. *Baseball's not out to get you. That's not even possible....*

She wanted—needed—someone to blame. Someone she could argue with. An inner impulse urged her to hash things out with God. But she resisted.

As a teen, Casey had turned to her heavenly Father when she'd struggled most with missing her earthly dad. Last winter, she had drawn comfort from God after her uncle's death. Most recently, she had immersed herself in the solace of his Word when she found herself alone and afraid, in a new town, feeling overwhelmed by new challenges. So far she had managed to trust him. But this time...this time it felt like he was asking too much.

Casey resisted the growing urge to lash out. What was the point in fighting with God? She knew what the result would be. God wasn't going to back down or be manipulated by her emotional outbursts. His will would be done. She simply had to give her burdens up and trust God with the results. Wasn't that what she kept telling the guys? Wasn't that her life motto?

Yet this time, she did not feel able to accept what life had dealt her. She didn't want to run from God. But she couldn't plead with him, either. This wasn't exactly a court of law....

The thought reminded her of a couple Bible verses that one of her college boyfriends, a law student, had been fond of quoting. "Isaiah 43:26!" he would proclaim. "'Put Me in remembrance; let us argue our case together.'" Or, "Isaiah 50:8! 'Who will contend with Me? Let us stand up to each other; Who has a case against Me? Let him draw near to Me.'"

"Oh, Tom!" Casey had responded once, laughing. "I don't think God meant those verses to be a special invitation for you to become a prosecuting attorney."

But the verses had stuck in her mind, and now she found herself repeating them, over and over. *"Let us argue our case together....Let us stand up to each other....Draw near to me...."*

"All right, God," she said finally, clearing her throat nervously. "I don't really know if that's the message you intended for me to get. But I'm going to try to...well, to draw near to you, like you said, and state my case." Kicking out of her kneeling position, she spun around and sat cross-legged, facing away from center field.

"I know you're God. And I want to trust you. But...it's hard. Right now, everything in me wants to yell out: 'Do you even care what's happening here? Is this your idea of a joke?' I know you're not playing with me, but I'm just so...mad!" Casey gestured wildly with her arms, as if to emphasize her point. "I wish you were physically here, so I could talk with you face-to-face. Although..." The absurdity of it struck her. "I guess if I saw you, the last thing I'd be worried about would be my love life, wouldn't it?"

As she expressed these thoughts and feelings out loud to her God, some of her anger began to fade.

"But...you know what I'm trying to say. You know this isn't just a simple crush, Father. I love Tucker. I really do. And I'm so *afraid* to love him, I hurt inside." Another tear escaped. "I don't know what I'll do if he goes away. I guess I'll cope. I always do—and you'll be there for me when I need you," she sighed. "But I don't just want to *cope* with life. I want to enjoy it! Sometimes I just want life to be...I don't know, *perfect,* I guess. It's silly...but I just wish life didn't have to be so *hard.*" By now, some of her tension had eased, and she was talking animatedly.

"I'm sorry I haven't talked with you about this before now, God. I've always said how important it is to trust you. It's not that I don't think you can handle this. Sometimes I just want to handle things myself. I guess I feel like if I don't face what's coming, it might not really happen. Talking to you always means facing things, and I just wasn't ready to do that yet." She paused.

"And…I guess I've been mad at you, too." She felt ridiculous saying such a thing. How could she, Casey Foster, have a right to be angry with God? "It feels terrible to say that. I almost expect to get struck with a bolt of lightning." She laughed nervously. "But I suppose I might as well tell you how I'm feeling, since you already know.

"I've tried really hard to serve you well, but it seems like life keeps getting harder and harder. I know that you're God, and you know better than I do what's best. On an intellectual level, I believe I shouldn't question you. But my selfish heart wants to beg you not to let me lose him, too." She squirmed uncomfortably as she began to feel in her back the effects of sitting on the hard earth.

"I'm sorry I've said these things. I'm sorry if I've hurt you." She paused. "Or maybe I've hurt you more by staying away… that's worse, isn't it? I'll try harder to trust you God," she said. "Please help my heart to understand what my head already knows: You are in control. You have a plan for me…a plan 'to prosper and not to harm' me. Isn't that what you said?"

Casey closed her eyes for a moment, then drew a long, deep breath.

"Okay, God. This one's yours. I know I'm pretty stubborn. I had no intention of giving this one up to you. But what else is there for me to do but be patient and trust you? Please help me to do that. I'm not so good at it on my own."

After she'd finished praying, Casey still felt miserable about Tucker. But at least she no longer had to deal with the added torture of running from God. She was glad that she had crossed that chasm before it became too wide.

Feeling emotionally spent, she climbed to her feet and picked up the bag. She looked inside…one ball left. She pulled it out, set the sack down again, and prepared to throw one last pitch. One last *quality* pitch.

With the ball clutched in her hands, Casey took her position, lining up her head and pivot foot with her center of gravity while drawing her hands close to her body. Keeping her thumbs down and her elbows up, she completed a full arc with her right arm, following through on a perfect hard sinker.

Casey placed her hands on her hips and smiled in satisfaction. That was better.

"Nice pitch, ace!" a familiar male voice called out.

Shocked at the sound, Casey turned.

"*Aaron?*"

The tall, sandy-haired man grinned and threw out his arms.

"Come here, sport, and give your little brother a big kiss."

∼ 21 ∽

For it's one, two, three strikes, 'You're out!' At the old ball game.
JACK NORWORTH, LYRICIST, 1908

A aron! What on earth are you doing here?" Casey blinked as if her eyes might be playing tricks on her.

Aaron grinned, thrusting his long, thin hands into the pockets of his baggy chino shorts. An ocean-green polo jersey hung low over his hips. His wavy, sand-colored locks fell across his forehead in a casual sweep, and his soft gray eyes reflected a gentle warmth.

"I came to see my sister, the hotshot baseball exec," he announced. "I've been waiting all summer for things to slow down at the vineyard so I could come up and visit you. It finally hit me last week that if I didn't do something soon, the baseball season would be over—and I knew you'd never forgive me if I missed it. I realized there would never be a convenient time, so I made an executive decision and chose an *inconvenient* one. I left Lutes in charge, and now…here I am! At your beck and call for an entire week, you lucky dog."

"But…I just talked with you on Thursday. You never said anything—"

"Of course not!" Aaron said triumphantly, throwing his arms around her in a crushing bear hug. Casey clung to him for a moment, thankful for the solid reassurance of his embrace. "I figured it would be much more fun to see the look on your face when I surprised you." He peered at her closely. "Although, I have to say, you don't look too good at all. Have you been sick?"

"It's nothing." Casey shook her head and averted her gaze. "How did you find me, anyway?"

"Oh, that was easy, my dear Watson," he quipped. "When you weren't at your house, I knew where to look. I lived with you long enough to know your usual haunts." He eyed her suspiciously. "Are you avoiding my question?"

"What question?"

"I asked if you've been sick. You don't really look like yourself."

"It's just a little stress, that's all," Casey insisted. "End of the season jitters. The Bachelor Party. Division play-offs. You know...the usual."

"Wow." Aaron let out a long, low whistle. "I'm impressed. And a little intimidated. All I've got to offer is a bunch of sour-grape stories."

"Ha, ha."

He took a moment to survey the stadium around them. "Yep, you've got a good thing here. I'm definitely jealous."

"Please. You hate baseball," she said, knowing her brother was only teasing.

Aaron tried to look offended. "I do *not* hate baseball. I hate dodgeball."

"Give me a break, Aaron. You used to boo at my Little League games."

"You're not ever going to let me forget that, are you?" he said in his best martyr tone. "I've told you before, I thought I was shouting at the other team." He shook his head in exaggerated dismay. "Some things never change. Already the president of a successful Napa Valley vineyard at the tender age of twenty-four, yet I don't get any respect."

"Oh, Aaron. Don't be such a *winer*," Casey teased.

"Ugh!" He rose to the challenge. "That one really hit *merlot* the belt."

"Stop it. You're making me *blush*."

The puns flew, as they often did between the Foster siblings, while Casey and Aaron gathered up her mitt and the scattered balls. As they walked back toward the clubhouse to put the equipment away, Casey tucked her free hand into the crook of his arm. "So, tell me, baby brother. How are things in Napa Valley, really? Are you liking the job as much as you claim?"

Aaron nodded enthusiastically. "Actually, I am. The power and responsibility are a little overwhelming at times, but it feels good to be in a position where I have a real impact on what's going on around me. The thing is, at first I wasn't really sure they needed me. As you know, after Uncle Edward got involved with the new team, his right-hand man, Frank Lutes, was more or less running things at the winery anyway. But it's too much for any one person to handle." He grinned. "Lutes says he's very impressed with me and my business background, and he's teaching me everything he knows about the industry."

"Sounds like he knows a good thing when he sees it," Casey said warmly as she unlocked the door to the equipment room.

"Well, I'm thankful," Aaron said. "You know, I've always wanted to do really well at something. This has been a very good experience for me."

"Yeah, but you've been doing great all along," Casey reminded him. "By the time you were twenty-two, you were practically running the entire financial division of a successful software development company. You can't tell me that didn't boost your ego."

"Oh, I'm sure it was a healthy enough shot in the arm," he

admitted. "But I have to say, this experience has been even greater. I don't know...maybe it has something to do with Dad running off on us, but I've always *really* wanted to live up to my potential." He shrugged. "Or maybe it's a guy thing."

The thought haunted her. *I'll have to ask Tucker about that.*

"What about you, superjock?" Aaron teased. "What's the latest at the Bachelor digs? Seems to me I remember you mentioning something about some outfielder, or was it a pitcher—?"

"Aaron!" she scolded him. "You know very well it was Tucker Boyd, so don't go pretending with me!"

"All right, all right!" He laughed. "So how *is* the incredible Mr. Boyd?"

"Actually...he's pitching pretty well," she said, hoping to sidestep the question.

"I didn't ask how he was pitching," he said pointedly. "I asked how he was *doing*—" Something in her look stopped him short. "Is there something I should know?"

Casey bit her lip. "We-ell—"

"Cas," he said fondly, "stop trying to be so self-sufficient. If there's something you need to talk about, then do it. You don't have to be totally in control all the time."

Knowing that no one else knew and understood her like Aaron did, Casey decided to let down her guard at last, and the words tumbled out in a rush as she explained the basic details of her situation.

As she was talking, she finished putting the balls and glove away and locked up her office. With that accomplished, she led her brother back out toward the parking lot.

"Coffee?" she suggested.

"Mmm...okay," he agreed. It was a sure sign that he understood the gravity of the situation. Under normal conditions, he would have teased Casey mercilessly about her caffeine addiction. "Let's leave the rental here," he said, patting his Ford

Tempo with one hand. "Want me to drive?"

Casey nodded. She felt like she might cry at any minute and was grateful for the opportunity to compose herself.

After giving Aaron directions to one of her favorite local cafes, she sat back against the Bronco's passenger seat and stared out the side window at the landmarks they passed.

"It sounds like you care about this guy an awful lot," Aaron observed, keeping his hands in his usual, quirky eleven and three position on the wheel. He followed Casey's directions to a T, turning onto Franklin and heading toward the downtown district.

"Yeah, I do." She had carefully avoided the word *love,* but she was sure that Aaron understood that it was implied.

"Well, then you may be looking at quite a mess," he suggested. Her little brother had always had a gift for understatement. "Then again, you might not be. Didn't you say that Clem himself wasn't sure that he was going to need Boyd?"

"Ye-es—"

"Well, then!" Aaron said, as if that settled it. "You might be wasting a good worry. If I were you, I'd keep my mouth shut until you know what Clem is going to decide. There's no sense in both you and Tucker getting all worked up about something that may never happen."

"But don't you think he has the right to know?" Casey protested.

"Know what? That there's an outside chance the Stars might want to use him?" Aaron made a rude raspberry noise with his lips. "That's not news. It's implied in him just *being* here."

Casey considered this. Wasn't what Aaron was suggesting really a form of dishonesty? Her brother had a good heart, but she wasn't used to taking his advice. As older sister, she'd generally been the one to guide *him.* Still, he did have a point.

"All right," she said. "What if I don't say anything now? And what if it turns out that the Stars *do* want him. What then?"

"Well, Cas, then I guess you'll have to let him go." Aaron spoke a little more gently. "I'll spare you the whole, 'if you love someone, set him free,' speech. But the truth of the matter is, he's not your personal property anyway. And if you think you can control things just by wishing hard enough for what you want, you're going to be in for a pretty big disappointment."

"Let him go, huh?" she repeated quietly.

"Only you can decide if that's what has to happen. It doesn't mean you don't care, Cas. It just means that you accept that there are things you can't control."

"You may be right."

As they pulled up in front of the restaurant, she gave her brother a watery smile. She loved him dearly, and his unexpected arrival was like an antidote for the anger that had begun to poison her spirit. She cast up a quick prayer of thanks to God for sending her much-needed reassurance of his love in what felt like her darkest hour.

Tucker gripped the wheel of his candy-apple red Miata and focused on the road ahead. His mouth was set in a grim line, and he drove in silence, not even thinking to turn on the classical music which rarely failed to calm his nerves.

He knew that something had happened to change Casey's heart. He just didn't know what that something was. Yesterday, everything had seemed fine, until about halfway through the game. Then, she had withdrawn, claiming that she wasn't feeling well. At first, he had taken her explanation at face value. But when he was unable to reach her today, either at home or at the park, he had become suspicious. That wasn't like Casey. Something was wrong, and she seemed determined to keep whatever it was from him.

Desperate for some clue, he had called several of the players and asked if they were aware of anything unusual that had happened the previous day. Only Gibby offered up a hint, when he casually mentioned that Casey had received a phone call in the dugout during the fourth inning. Gib hadn't known, however, who had been on the other end of the line. It was during that time, Tucker remembered, that he had first noticed the change in Casey's attitude.

He downshifted in traffic and pointed the Mazda in the direction of the stadium. She had to be somewhere, and he was going to find her, if he had to personally check out every one of her favorite hangouts. He'd already eliminated her house as a possibility, and he doubted that she was at the ballpark; if she'd been there, wouldn't she have picked up the phone? But he had to start somewhere. Hopefully she had been there earlier and had left a clue.

He turned the car onto the street that led to the stadium, and his heart leaped as he recognized the vehicle approaching him from the opposite direction. Casey's Bronco! He eased his foot down on the gas pedal, giving his engine more juice, and leaned forward with his arm half-raised, poised to wave furiously. He peered into the driver's side window, a grin plastered on his face, and tried to make eye contact with....

A strange man.

He blinked. It wasn't Casey's Bronco at all.

But then, in an instant, he realized that it was. His eyes flickered to the passenger seat, where she sat, her head tipped back against the headrest, a blank expression on her face as she gazed out the side window.

Then the Bronco was gone.

Instantly, feelings of rage rose in Tucker's chest. What was going on? Who was that guy? Was he what she'd needed "time" for last night? Was he the reason Casey had been avoiding him?

His initial impulse was to make a U-turn and follow the two to wherever they were headed, but he forced himself to stay calm.

Slowly, his feelings of anger turned into a dull ache in his heart. His relationship with Casey had seemed to be progressing perfectly, but perhaps things weren't as ideal as he thought. He'd never really asked her what she wanted out of the relationship; he simply assumed that she wanted what he did. He'd never told her that he saw things continuing to move forward for them.

He'd never told her that he loved her.

Stung by a sense of regret, he played back memories of all the times when he could have spoken up, but hadn't. He had wanted to take things slowly. He'd wanted the moment to be right.

And he'd waited too long.

Overcome with remorse, Tucker absently made a left at the next block and prepared to circle back toward his apartment. There was nothing he could do now.

Or was there?

A faint glimmer of hope began to flicker. Perhaps the guy was just a casual acquaintance. It wasn't likely that she would turn the wheel of her beloved Bronco over to someone she didn't completely trust, but it wasn't impossible, either. Maybe she was still feeling sick, and the man was helping her run some important errands....

The excuse sounded weak, but it was better than nothing. And he needed all the confidence he could muster if he was going to make one final attempt to win Casey back.

He'd let her take the "time" she needed today. But tonight, after the game, he was going to settle things once and for all. It was time Casey knew that he loved her.

And he wasn't going to let her go without a fight.

Casey's heart fluttered as Tucker stepped into the dugout. She had managed to avoid seeing him until just before the start of the game. But there was no avoiding him now.

Across the crowd of players, the look he gave her was poignant and searching, and it was all she could do not to run across the dugout and throw her arms around him.

At the sight of his anguished face, her heart sank, and she realized that the time she had selfishly claimed for herself had taken a toll on him. This made her more determined than ever to follow through on the decision she had made that afternoon. Her brother was right. Until she had reason to believe that the Stars actually intended to call Tucker up, she would focus on what they had, and not on the fact that it might be lost.

She forced a smile onto her face and stepped across the dugout to his side.

"Hi," she said.

"Hi." His voice betrayed a mixture of confusion, suffering, and what sounded like a hint of determination.

"I missed you today," she said softly.

"Did you?" Casey thought she saw a flush of pleasure and relief on his face.

"And last night."

"I missed you, too." He reached out and pulled her gently into his arms.

"Hey, hey now!" Cage said, walking by. "No unnecessary P.D.A.s, please."

Casey smiled, thankful for the humor, which helped to ease the tension of the moment. "Sorry, Eddie. We'll try to keep our public displays of affection to a minimum." As she pulled herself from Tucker's arms, she noticed that he had held her a bit more tightly than usual, and that he seemed inordinately unwilling to let her go.

"I think we should talk after the game," he said in a low voice.

Casey nodded. "All right," she said warily. She had decided to leave her uncertainties behind her. But Tucker clearly needed an explanation for her sudden change in behavior, and she still wasn't sure what she was going to say.

Suddenly, she remembered her brother, watching the game from the stands. "I'll have a surprise for you," she said brightly, in an attempt to lighten the mood. She was looking forward to Aaron and Tucker meeting. She was certain that the two most important men in her life would like each other.

"I'll be waiting," Tucker promised her. As he turned away and stepped out of the dugout to continue his warm-ups, Casey felt her shoulders tense.

It was going to be a very long game.

By the bottom of the fifth inning, the Bachelors had already scored a three-run lead over the visiting Mustangs, despite the fact that Tucker was struggling slightly on the mound. Casey knew he was distracted, and she felt guilty for that, but she was also glad to see that he was managing to keep his personal feelings from completely shaking up his game.

She watched as he threw a steady mix of fastballs, sliders, change-ups, and curves. From time to time, one caught a bit too much of the plate, but he was fairly consistent. If he was able to maintain, they should have the game, and a slot in the division play-offs, sewn up.

Behind her the telephone rang once. Then twice. Then a third time.

Casey listened, unable to move, and the roar of the crowd faded away until she could hear only the steady, insistent ringing in her ears.

211

A couple of players threw her glances of irritation as she stood motionless beside the phone, letting its annoying sound go unchecked. Finally, Holmes walked over and picked up the receiver.

"It's for you, Casey," he said a moment later, just as she'd known he would. Flashing her a strange look, he handed her the receiver and walked away.

"Hi, Clem," she spoke into the mouthpiece.

"Hi, kiddo." He didn't even ask how she'd known it was him.

"You need him, don't you," she said simply, but it was not a question.

Clem let out a heavy sigh. "It's not lookin' good here. Lopez is out for the rest of the season, and I need another backup. Sorry to steal your best man away before the play-offs...."

"...but that's the way the game goes," she finished for him. "I know. When do you want him?"

"Have him get a ticket for Tuesday. I know it's short notice..."

Casey sank to the bench as her head began to spin. Three days. That wasn't enough time. She couldn't possibly let him go that quickly....

"Three days. You got it," she heard herself saying. That had been her decision, hadn't it? To let Tucker go, like Aaron had suggested. Besides, she really didn't have any other choice.

Feelings of loss overwhelmed her. She couldn't bear losing another man to the game. She knew that Tucker would choose baseball over her. He'd be crazy not to. In her head, she heard the echo of the words her father had uttered more than once: *"Don't worry, baby. I'll be back."*

He probably meant it, too, she thought, giving him the benefit of the doubt. But eventually, he'd be gone for good.

I don't want it to be like that this time, she thought. *I don't want to be waiting for Tucker to come back.* The receiver hung, unheeded, in her hand as Clem rattled off details that she didn't hear. *I want this to be a clean break. No false expectations. No added pressure of trying to make something impossible work.*

Suddenly, she knew what she had to do. Although she'd never articulated the thought, it had been hovering just below her consciousness ever since Friday night.

Tucker would never be able to concentrate fully in Phoenix if he knew she was miserable in Bend. And she didn't want him to consume the energy he so desperately needed to invest in the game worrying about a relationship that really wasn't going anywhere anyway. So the best, most loving, thing she could do for him was cut all ties completely.

Telling Clem she would call him the next day to make arrangements, Casey hung up the phone and stumbled back to her office to collect her thoughts. She needed a plan. She had always been a terrible liar. But this time, her poker face had to be perfect.

Tucker's future depended on it.

"Gibby said you wanted me to meet you here."

Startled, Casey spun around from her position at the window. Tucker stood in the doorway, looking as attractive as ever in faded jeans and a light blue-and-white-checked seersucker shirt. More than ever, she wanted to run to him and throw herself into his arms.

"Hi," she said, holding her position. "Good game tonight."

Tucker shrugged. It was clear that he wasn't here to talk about the game.

"Can we talk?" he asked.

Casey nodded. "I think we should." Walking to the front of her desk, she glanced at the chair across from it. "Would you like to have a seat?"

Her stiffness did not go unnoticed. Tucker moved toward the chair, choosing to stand behind it. Casey hopped up onto the edge of her desk.

"I know what you're going to say," she began.

"Oh, you think you do," he said, with a bit of an edge.

Casey paused. She could hear a hint of anger creeping into his voice.

"Ye-es, I think I do." Tucker's eyes were penetrating. She looked away. "You've noticed that I've been acting strangely, and you want an explanation. I don't blame you." She focused on a black smudge on the wall, remembering the time when the rubber of Holmes's shoe had made contact during one of the players' unsanctioned games of "Keep Away."

"I've been thinking a lot the past few days. From the start, I've been uncomfortable with the idea of dating one of my players. It feels...inappropriate, and—" She drew a deep breath. "It's getting harder for me. I just don't feel like it's worth the feelings of discomfort. I...I don't see things working out for us." She forced herself to look him squarely in the face. "I'm sorry, but I don't want to see you anymore."

His expression remained blank. For a moment, it appeared as though he had not heard her at all. Casey held her breath as understanding dawned on him, and all the color drained from his face. He opened his lips as if to speak, but no sound came forth.

For a moment, he stood clutching the back of the chair. Then he turned and, without a word, strode to the opposite side of the room. At the door, he stopped, turned, and gave her one last, unbelieving stare.

"Well, that was certainly some 'surprise,'" he said hoarsely.

Casey stared at his cryptic choice of words, not catching his meaning. Then it hit her. She had completely forgotten about introducing him to Aaron, who probably was right now wandering around the dugout looking for her.

Tucker licked his lips and seemed about to speak once more. Then he snapped his mouth shut, turned away, and walked out the door, taking Casey's heart with him.

~ 22 ~

It breaks your heart. It is designed to break your heart. The game begins in the spring, when everything else begins again, and it blossoms in the summer, filling the afternoons and evenings, and then as soon as the chill rains come, it stops and leaves you to face the fall alone.

A. BARTLETT GIAMATTI, COMMISSIONER OF BASEBALL

SUNDAY, AUGUST 10

Casey watched the pastor's lips move, but he might have been speaking a foreign language, for all she comprehended of his words. To her left, Aaron sat, intently listening to the message. At her right, the polished wooden pew was empty. For the past month, Tucker had come to church with her every Sunday. But this morning, he had not shown up. She understood. It would have been awkward for them both if he'd come.

While the pastor began to wrap up his message about the Great Commission, Casey's thoughts continued to drift back to the previous night's confrontation. *Please God, help Tucker,* she prayed silently. *And please help me. I think I did the right thing, but I'm not sure. I know I meant to do the right thing. Please give me some reassurance. Anything, Lord...* Her mind was racing. It was impossible to feel any sense of peace.

She sat up straight and, resisting the urge to stretch, tried to focus her thoughts on the sermon, picking up on the pastor's words as he read the final verses from the book of Matthew:

"…and lo, I am with you always, even to the end of the age."

"Lo, I am with you." Casey opened up her Bible and read the words again. *"Lo, I am with you."* The words spoke directly to her.

I know you are, Lord, she prayed. *Thank you.*

He knew what was going on. He was with her.

She could rest in that.

Casey sat in her office, not even pretending to work. There wasn't any point. She was just killing time until Aaron got back from running errands, anyway. While she was waiting, she conducted a mental review of what she planned to say to Tucker the next time she saw him.

When he stormed through the door of her office at a quarter after two, she wasn't surprised. Casey had never questioned whether or not he would come looking for her. She had simply wondered about his timing.

"We need to talk," Tucker said roughly. Casey could hear the strain in his voice. His dark hair was rumpled, as if he had combed it with his fingers, and his faded gray sweats and spruce-colored T-shirt looked like they had been slept in.

She stood and mustered up all her courage to speak. "We talked last night," she told him calmly, but her heart was racing.

"No. *You* talked last night," Tucker corrected, just as she had known he would.

This is unfolding just as you expected. Just stick to your plan.

Casey sat back down, not at her usual, comfortable desktop perch, but behind the desk in her tattered faux-leather office chair. Tucker made no move to sit, but stormed around the room, his athletic shoes squeaking against the vinyl tiles.

"You didn't give me a chance to say anything last night," he began, but Casey cut him off.

"You didn't try."

He spun on one foot and stared at her incredulously. "How could I have said anything? Unlike you, I hadn't had a chance to think things through; I just got blindsided. It doesn't make any *sense.*" He was looking desperate now, and Casey resisted every urge to break down and tell him the truth. "You never said anything about this whole owner/player issue before. If it's awkward for you, we can always—"

"Tucker." Casey folded her arms resolutely across her chest. "I don't want to argue about this. I've made up my mind."

His dark eyes flashed. "You've made up your mind? You've made up *your* mind?" he spat out. "What about my mind? What about my *feelings?*"

"Tucker, I care more about your feelings than you realize."

"That's rather hard to believe!"

"I'm sorry. I'm not doing this to hurt you."

"Well, that's too bad, 'cause that sure is the result."

She fidgeted with the fabric of the dress she had worn to church that morning, the same pale yellow jacquard she had worn to the auction. "I said I'm sorry." The scene was surreal, like something out of her worst nightmare.

Tucker crossed the room and leaned heavily on the desk in front of her. "Casey, please. Surely you're not saying that you didn't feel what I felt all along? You started out as my friend, perhaps the closest friend I've had in years. And you quickly became the woman I adore. I know relationships can be hard. But we're both strong people. We can work this through—"

"Tucker, don't." Casey could not take much more. If she did not put an end to this, she would crumble. "You're making this harder than it has to be. I was afraid it would be like this, which is exactly why I did what I did this morning."

He stepped back and regarded her with growing dismay. "What did you do?" he asked, his voice heavy with dread.

Drawing upon all her strength, Casey met his troubled hazel eyes with a steady gaze. *Those are still the most incredible eyes I've ever seen.* "I called Al Clements and talked with him about your progress." She paused for dramatic effect. "He thinks you're ready, Tucker. They've had a couple of injuries on the team and they can use you." She tried to sound pleased, but the words came out low and strained. "You're going back to the show."

"The show." Tucker repeated the words dully, as if he did not know what they meant. "I can't believe you did this." He turned away. Casey could not tell whether the statement was one of appreciation or anger.

He began to pace. "You want to get rid of me pretty bad, don't you?" he threw out angrily.

"Tucker, that's not it—"

"Then what, Casey?" he exploded. "This isn't about me being one of your players, is it?"

"Of course it is."

"No. No." He shook his head vehemently and quickened his step. "It's something else, and I know what that something is."

"All right, then," Casey said patiently. "Tell me."

He stopped pacing. "You've met someone else."

"What?" The accusation stunned her. "You're joking, right?"

"Not even close."

She tried to imagine what he could mean. "Who? One of the guys on the team?"

"No."

"But, Tucker," Casey protested, "I spend every waking minute here at the ballpark. Just where and when do you suggest I would have had the time or the opportunity to meet anyone?"

"I have no idea. But it's the only thing that makes sense."

"I know this is hard, and I don't blame you for feeling confused. But I *promise* you this is not about someone else."

"Fine," he spat out in disgust. "Don't tell me the truth."

"Tucker!" Casey wanted to argue him down. But how could she convince him that she wasn't lying when that was exactly what she was doing? "I guess you can believe what you want to believe. It doesn't matter, anyway. I can't see you anymore—"

"You mean 'won't.'" He spoke bitterly. The fire in his voice was dying.

"—and besides, you'll be leaving Tuesday for Phoenix. We'll send on your things," she told him. Her eyes pleaded with him to accept what had to be. "This doesn't have to be a bad thing, Tucker. Try to look ahead. Forget about you and me. It was fun—a summer fling," she lied. "And summer flings can be wonderful. But then the winter comes and they're over. You've got an opportunity to move on to something now that will last more than one season."

Feeling an urgent desire to close the gap between them, she rose from behind her desk and went around to stand before him. The move very nearly backfired on her, as she felt overwhelmed by the desire to fall into his arms and confess everything.

"You've finally learned to *love* baseball. To play with your heart. Remember? Take that with you. Share it with your new team...your fans. I promise I'll be one of them." Her voice trembled, and she turned away.

"You know, I don't think I'll ever understand what happened here," he said brokenly. "From the very beginning, I felt connected to you, Casey. I was drawn to your laughter, your craziness, your compassion for people...including me.

"You brought hope and light back into my life. You reminded me of the things that matter most. Nothing will ever be the same again. You've become a part of me, and I'll carry you in my heart always." He reached out with arms that shook and pulled her into his embrace.

"I never got a chance to tell you that I love you," he whis-

220

pered against the softness of her hair. "It seems pitiful to say so after the fact, but I do. I do love you, Casey. As much as any man ever loved a woman, and with emotions far greater than anything I thought I had the capacity to feel."

In her mind, Casey reached up and smoothed out the worry lines on his brow. In reality, she kept her hands motionless, barely touching the soft fabric of his shirt at the sides of his waist.

"I think we could have made it," Tucker told her softly. "Life's hard, and it takes two people who are totally committed to one another to make it through the storms. I don't know why you don't want to go through them with me. Maybe there just wasn't enough time for you to see that I am sincere. But I mean it, Casey. I love you, and I always will."

Lovingly, he drew his trembling fingers through her hair. Beneath her cheek, Casey could feel the rapid pounding of his heartbeat. She lifted her face to his and watched with wide eyes as his face drew close to hers....

The sound of loud whistling rang out from the hallway, startling them both.

"...buy me some peanuts and Cracker Jacks, I don't care if I *never* get back!" Aaron sang out cheerfully and off-key. "Hey, Cas. Betcha thought I'd got lost, but I'm back! I was thinking that maybe this afternoon we could—whoops!" By the time he entered the room, Tucker and Casey were standing several feet apart, but it was clear that he knew he had interrupted a very private moment. "Whoa, sorry! Bad timing. Don't mind me, I'll just—"

Tucker stared at Aaron with hatred in his eyes. "I knew it!"

Casey looked at him in dismay. "What is it?" Still caught up in the emotion of the moment they had just shared, she had trouble clearing her head enough to understand what he was saying.

"It's *him*, isn't it?"

Aaron looked at Tucker like he was a raving lunatic. "Yes, it's me. What about me?"

Tucker ignored him. "I should have known better than to come here and try to work things out," he said to Casey. "It's obvious what's going on."

She was still trying to catch up. "What? What do you mean?"

"Just forget it!"

"But, Tucker—"

"Don't waste your breath." The look in his eyes was that of a man who had been mortally wounded. "I hope you two will be very happy together." He stormed to the door, giving Aaron a look of anger as he passed.

Understanding finally dawned on her. "No! Tucker! It's not what you think. Please, wait—" But he was already halfway down the hall.

It was just on her lips to say, "Tucker, it's Aaron! He's my brother!" but she stopped herself. Wasn't this the goal? Her plan had worked. She had wanted to convince him to make a clean break before leaving for Phoenix. Hadn't she?

After hearing his declaration of love, she wasn't so sure.

As her heart deliberated, Tucker disappeared around the end of the hallway, and Casey realized that she had made her choice. The pain she felt was nearly unbearable, but dragging things out would simply make matters worse.

Aaron came up beside her and laid an arm around her shoulders. "Wow! That was ugly," he said with his gift for understatement.

With tears coursing down her cheeks, Casey allowed him to draw her into his arms, as she began to quietly mourn the loss of the greatest love of her life.

23

It ain't over 'til it's over.
YOGI BERRA

FRIDAY, AUGUST 15

I hate 'old maids.'" With her stocking feet stretched out in front of her on the Cambridge sofa, her slouch socks living up to their name, Casey glared at the unpopped kernels of corn left in her blue ceramic bowl. She'd already lost the one man she could have loved for a lifetime. She didn't need her snack foods to remind her that she was likely to spend the rest of her days alone.

"But I *like* being alone," she told herself grumpily, poking idly through the golden seeds.

Actually, there was some truth to her protest.

Casey had never felt the need to "pair up" like the animals on the ark. She knew that there were plenty of benefits to having a boyfriend; not the least of which, in her eyes, was the added bonus of having a built-in tennis partner. But while kisses were pleasant, and having a regular sporting companion convenient, it had seemed a high price to pay for all the heartache men and women went through. Long ago, she'd decided that she would be perfectly happy spending her life as a single person, if that's what life should bring.

That was, until Tucker Boyd came along.

It wasn't that she needed someone—just anyone—to fill the emptiness in her heart. She wanted Tucker. She missed Tucker. Over the past five days, she'd dreamed up countless fantasies, all of them centering around the primary objective of seeing him just one more time.

Like scenes from a looping videotape, visions of their last interaction played over and over in her mind, accompanied by the questions that continued to torment her: Did she make the right decision? Should she have gone after him? Did he really love her? Could they have worked things out?

Even now, she longed to call him and explain. Yet she remained convinced that Tucker would be better off with the Stars, and with each day that passed, she knew that chances for a reconciliation grew increasingly slim. She'd hurt him deeply; she had seen it in his eyes. He said he loved her, and she believed he meant it. But would he really be able to forgive her for what she'd put him through? Casey had never experienced a love that strong. She dared not even hope it could exist.

She set the popcorn bowl aside and reached for the remote control. Thankfully, Aaron had gone for a long ride on her mountain bike, so she would be able to watch the game in peace—Casey had been telling the truth about him hating baseball. She snapped on the set ten full minutes before coverage began. Today would mark Tucker's debut as a pitcher for Phoenix, and she did not want to miss even a moment of the broadcast. Throwing a soft angora throw over her bare legs, she settled in to watch the game.

The program had just begun when the announcers flashed up on the screen a team photo of Tucker—looking tired, Casey thought—and gave a brief summation of his pitching credits. The sight of his picture caused her pulse to race. But it was the live shot of him, warming up in the bull pen, that caused her the most anxiety. Casey jumped off the couch and pressed her face close to the screen, searching for any clues as to how he might be feeling, but his expression revealed only deep concentration. Tucker appeared to have only one thing on his mind—his pitching.

She scrambled back onto the couch and nervously gnawed on the unpopped kernels of corn until the game began.

Casey enjoyed every aspect of baseball: each call, each swing, each mind-numbing detail that caused casual onlookers to rank the sport just slightly more enjoyable than a trip to the dentist. But tonight, the announcers' endless chatter nearly drove her out of her mind, and she could not wait for Tucker to come onto the field.

To her surprise, she did not have to wait long. She had expected them to bring him in later in the game. But apparently player injuries had taken an even greater toll than she'd realized, for Tucker was brought in right at the start, in the very first inning.

Casey held her breath. She wanted so much for him to do well. All the suffering from the past week was forgotten as she focused on one thought: *Please, God, be with Tucker. Help him to relax, to play from his heart.*

She noticed that he did, indeed, look relaxed on the field. The weariness she'd seen captured in his team picture was gone. As he took to the mound, Tucker smiled at the crowd that was wildly cheering and shouting his name. In the background, Casey saw a large, homemade sign hung from the stadium wall, upon which a fan had printed the words: WELCOME BACK TO THE 'BIG TIME' BOYD!

Tucker waved graciously, acknowledging the fans' support with a humble nod, then bowed his head for a moment. *Collecting his thoughts,* Casey thought, *or praying—or both.*

Within minutes, he was ready to begin. His first two pitches were solid: the same sinking fastball that had taken her by surprise at the charity game, and a perfect backdoor slider. The third was a curveball that hit high and inside. Although he shouldn't have even tried for it, the batter was anxious and clipped it. She watched in amazement as the ball flew straight to Tucker, who scooped it up neatly and drilled it to first for an easy first out.

The crowd went wild, and Casey felt a warm rush of pleasure and pride.

The rest of the game was more of the same, and at the end the score was seven to three, in favor of the Stars.

After the final inning, the network sports anchor directed viewers to stay tuned for an interview with the Most Valuable Player of the night: none other than Tucker "Big Time" Boyd.

Throughout the seemingly endless commercial break, Casey sat chewing her nails and hugging her knees, sitting inches from the screen of the television set. Finally, after what felt like hours, postgame coverage began. After listening to one particularly annoying analyst drone on endlessly about Tucker's performance, Casey finally found herself gazing upon his dear face as the network cut to a live, on-the-field interview.

"Tucker, congratulations on what has turned out to be a *spectacular* return to major league baseball!" shouted the enthusiastic interviewer, Lou Espinoza.

"Thanks, Lou," Tucker said warmly. "The reception I've received here in Phoenix has been incredible."

"And so it should be!" Espinoza flashed the camera a stereotypical car-salesman grin.

He turned back to Boyd and managed to rein in his energy long enough to ask one question without shouting. "Tucker, it's been almost two years since your rotator cuff injury first took you off the field. You spent over a year in rehab, then struggled with inconsistent pitching until the middle of this season, which you played with the double-A, minor league Bend Bachelors. To what do you attribute your phenomenal and rather sudden improvement?"

Tucker looked straight into the camera, giving Casey a clear view of his hypnotizing, gold-flecked eyes. "Well, Lou, there are a number of factors," he said. "I had the honor and privilege of working with Don Shelton, who I believe to be the best pitching coach in baseball today."

Then his expression became more serious. But, Casey thought, he didn't look sad or angry—only thoughtful. She leaned in close, wanting to catch every inflection, every nuance of his voice.

"I also made a wonderful friend who helped me work through some emotional and spiritual issues," Tucker said warmly. "This person helped me overcome obstacles that had been plaguing me for years. I'm certain that without her help, I wouldn't be here today. I owe her a tremendous debt of thanks, which I plan to repay the next time I see her—" His smile grew wide. "Which I hope will be very soon."

Casey's heart leaped in her chest.

"I'd say the third and most important factor in my improvement, Lou, would be my relationship with God. I'd been running from him for most of my life, but over the past few months I've been able to build a solid friendship with him." He laughed. "Don't get me wrong. I'm not suggesting that God is rewarding me for praying more, or anything like that. But, really, a lot of my pitching problems had to do with my lack of inner peace. That's something I've been able to find lately, and it has impacted every area of my life. Pitching just happens to be a part of that."

"I see." Espinoza looked at the camera uncertainly, as if unsure of how to handle the moment. In a moment, though, the cheesy grin and loud voice were back. "Well…uh…can you tell us, Big Time, what your plans are? Can the fans expect to see you in a Stars' uniform next year, or will you be considering other offers?"

"Well, actually, Lou," Tucker said, a slow smile spreading across his features, "I'm in the process of making alternate plans."

"Alternate…plans?" The interviewer looked confused.

"You see, if things go the way I'm hoping they will, I won't be playing in the majors next year at all."

Espinoza nearly dropped his microphone.

Casey stared at Tucker's image on the set.

"That's right," Tucker explained, his gold eyes sparkling. "You see, I've been playing baseball for a long time now, but I'm still pretty new at being in love. And I'm hoping for some time to give it more practice."

Casey's jaw dropped, and the room began to spin.

"The truth is, I love baseball more now than I ever have before." Tucker gave the camera a mischievous wink. "But I have to admit, these days I've got a whole different kind of diamond on my mind."

~ 24 ~

Think about each pitch like you think about women, then select one which is particularly appealing.
TOMMY LASORDA, MINOR LEAGUE MANAGER, 1970

SATURDAY, AUGUST 16

It was the perfect day for a Bachelor Party.

With great satisfaction Casey surveyed the stands, filled to overflowing with eager fans screaming wildly for the hometown team. Men, women, and children alike played with kazoos and other party favors that had been scattered throughout the seats. On the field, her favorite high school marching band was playing up the theme of the evening; at the moment they were wandering aimlessly to the beat of "Get Me to the Church on Time." Even Barry Bachelor had gotten into the spirit of things, exchanging his tails for a groom's tuxedo. Casey waved at the mascot, who was running around flirting with various individuals in the audience. She laughed. Ross Chambers had been one of the key factors in making the season a success. She'd have to think of some special way to thank him later.

In the dugout, emotions were running high as the players prepared to compete in their last regular-season game. Casey checked her watch. The band was over its allotted time by about ten minutes, but the crowd didn't seem to mind. Besides, things were just getting good: One gawky percussionist had dropped a drumstick and was turning around in circles, like a dog chasing his tail, trying to find it.

She grabbed the walkie-talkie that was her only source of communication with the fireworks crew. "Hey, Arthur? I think we're running about fifteen minutes behind. Will that work?"

"Check."

It seemed as though everything was falling right into place.

Everything except Tucker.

Casey wrinkled her brow and scanned the stands one more time. It had been over twenty-four hours since his much-celebrated interview, and she still hadn't heard a peep out of the man who suddenly had "a whole different kind of diamond" on his mind.

From the moment she'd heard his words, Casey had been overcome with joy. She didn't know how or why...but for some reason, Tucker had forgiven her. And he was coming home.

Suddenly, the issues that had frightened her did not seem so insurmountable anymore. She hadn't asked Tucker to give up anything. He had made his own choice.

He had chosen her.

After the broadcast yesterday, her phone had rung off the hook with calls from friends who had seen the interview and suspected that Casey was the woman who had changed Tucker's life. Her team members had been the worst—or the best, depending on one's perspective—with their teasing remarks and good wishes. Unfortunately, none of the calls had been from Tucker.

At first, she had resisted the urge to dial the phone. She desperately longed to hear the sound of his voice, however, and soon was ready to give in—but then realized she didn't even have his new number. There was nothing to do but wait. He had practically proposed to her on national television. He knew how to reach her. It wouldn't be long.

When she hadn't heard from him by bedtime, Casey had become quite alarmed. Finally, in desperation, this morning, she had called Clem.

"Well, if it isn't the woman who stole away my best pitcher!" he groused. But in spite of the loss he had suffered, he seemed genuinely pleased for Casey. "I don't know what you did to that man, but he's sure a lot happier than I've ever seen him. You've got a good thing there, kiddo," he said.

"I know I do, Clem," she'd said, although by this time she was beginning to wonder. "Say, I was just thinking…in all the excitement, I didn't find out where Tucker is staying." She crossed her fingers guiltily, but it wasn't exactly a lie.

"Well, he was at the Hilton, last I heard," Clem said thoughtfully. "But, of course, you know he headed out this morning?"

"He—oh, of course. Where's my head?" Casey felt like a total idiot. She wasn't even sure that Tucker was headed back to Oregon, but she could hardly ask Clem that! "Well, thanks for being so understanding." She'd rung off as quickly as she could.

And so, Tucker remained at large, and Casey remained the target of incessant teasing.

"Where's your boyfriend?"

"Gee, Casey, where is he? Did you scare him off already?"

And worst one of all: "I can't believe the guy would miss his own Bachelor Party!"

Casey threw a glance at the field. The marching band was finally shuffling off, clearing the way for the next part of the show to begin. She was just about to cue the fireworks when she spied Barry Bachelor waving furiously at her.

She shook her head no and pointed to the walkie-talkie in

her hand. Ross knew the fireworks were next on the schedule. He must have forgotten.

When the frantic gestures continued, Casey realized that something must be wrong.

"Hey, guys," she spoke into the radio in her hand, "I've got another holdup. Wait on those fireworks until I give you a cue."

"Roger."

By the time she'd made it across the field, she was completely out of breath.

"What's the matter, Ross?" she panted.

But the giant-headed mascot just danced a little jig.

The audience roared.

Still gasping for breath, Casey threw him an odd look. "What on earth is the matter with you?"

Barry gave a little hop-skip, turned, and pointed dramatically at the marching band, which had gathered at the side of the field. Immediately, the group broke into a toe-tapping version of "Shall We Dance?"

For the second time in as many days, Casey found herself speechless, with her mouth hanging open, as the mascot seized her by the arms and began to spin her crazily around the field. Up and down they flew, she in her ankle-length georgette skirt and white sweater, and he in his enormous head. Several times, she tried to protest. But his grip was so firm, and their velocity so great, she could neither catch her breath nor break away.

At long last, the song ended when the drummer lost his rhythm and the rest of the band helplessly followed suit. Her head spinning, Casey looked at the creature incredulously.

"What's going on? Have you lost your mind?"

Barry shook his head fervently, making the pupils of his huge plastic eyes rattle. Casey watched in amazement as he bowed low from the hips, doffed his top hat to her, then lowered himself on one knee and tipped up his big felt head with its great, smirking red mouth.

"No," came a muffled voice from inside the creature's body. "But I *have* lost my heart."

The entire stadium howled in amusement, then erupted into deafening cheers as Barry Bachelor reached up with his two oversized hands and pulled off his gigantic head, revealing a very smug-looking Tucker Boyd.

"Tucker!" Tears of joy and laughter sprang to Casey's eyes. "I was so worried that you wouldn't come! I thought maybe you'd changed your mind. I wouldn't have blamed you if you had—"

A large felt finger fell across her lips, silencing her. "Shh, sweetheart. Of course I came back. Did you really think you could get rid of me that easily?"

"Oh, Tucker!" she cried unhappily. "I didn't ever want to get rid of you! I was just so *afraid.* I couldn't bear for you to leave me. But I couldn't bring myself to ask you to stay. It wouldn't have been fair to ask you to make that choice—"

"You didn't have to ask," he assured her. "I made it on my own."

"But, Tucker! You must feel like you've lost so much!"

His eyes met hers. "Only if I've lost you."

Casey threw herself into his soft, fuzzy embrace. "I'm so sorry! I never meant to hurt you…and then I lied! Oh, can you ever forgive me? Everything just got so out of control! I've been haunted by memories of my father leaving us—"

"I know," he said, drawing her closer.

Casey looked at him, wide-eyed. "You know? How could you—?"

"I knew from the beginning that there was something else behind your decision." Tucker's arms rested, heavy and comfortable, against her waist. "You're a terrible liar, you know," he said fondly. "You didn't even cover up your tracks. Do you know how easy it was to find out what was really going on? Once I got to Phoenix, I learned from Clem that it was his idea, not yours, for me to move up to the Stars. I also found out that the offer had come the day before you broke it to me—explaining your sudden change of heart."

He gave her a sheepish grin. "I'm afraid Gordy 'accidentally' slipped me a few hints about your dad." Tucker's expression softened. "He also set me straight on that new 'boyfriend' of yours." He squeezed her tightly around the waist. "I'm sorry, sweetheart. I shouldn't have doubted you."

Casey shook her head emphatically. "I don't blame you a bit! After everything I put you through, how could you have trusted me?" She looked at him with question in her eyes. "But, Tucker, are you sure you aren't going to mind leaving the majors?"

His smile was tender. "After all the time you spent convincing me it's people and God that matter, telling me that it's only a game...how could you think that I would let something like this come between us?" He hugged her fiercely.

"Casey, it's you I love. Anything else that comes is just a bonus. Maybe in Phoenix I could have been a star." His eyes searched hers. "But it is here in your arms that I feel safe."

She wrapped her arms tightly around his neck. "Will you really come back?" she asked happily.

"If you'll take an old has-been major leaguer like me," Tucker joked.

"Seriously, though," she said, snuggling her face into the warm hollow of his neck. "Are you really going to be happy playing double-A ball for the rest of your career?"

"Perhaps not," Tucker admitted. "Although, being a big star was always my dad's dream, not mine. This has been a good year for me. I'm enjoying the minor leagues a lot more than I ever did the bigs. Anyway," he said, looking at her tenderly, "this is an important time for us; I don't want to spend the next season away from you, traipsing all over the country. For now, I believe I'm right where God wants me. Although..." his voice trailed off as he began to consider his options. "I think I still have some pretty good pitching left in me. Maybe in a year or two you'll want to try sports reporting again and I'll want to go back to the majors. I may even take a shot at coaching; I liked working with the younger guys the past few months. We'll see."

He reached into a pocket hidden within the massive costume and pulled out a tiny, black velvet box. "I'm warning you, though," he said lightly, "this means I probably won't stay a Bachelor forever."

Laughing happily, Casey slipped the diamond onto her finger and smiled back at her love. "I'm glad to hear you say it. 'Cause that's what I was counting on."

With that, the man she adored wrapped big floppy arms around her slender body and tipped her head backward for a slow, tender kiss.

At exactly that moment, the sky exploded in bursts of fiery red, brilliant orange, and shimmering yellows, blues, and greens as the marching band kicked into the opening bars of "Louie, Louie," a song that was rapidly rising higher and higher in Casey's esteem.

From the stands above, two fireworks engineers surveyed the evening's show with the greatest of satisfaction.

"Now *that* was a cue for fireworks," Arthur said knowingly, "if I *ever* saw one."

Dear Reader,

Believe it or not, I've never really been a big baseball fan. It's nothing against the sport itself. It's just that I'm...well, a klutz. As a kid, whenever I found myself in the horrifying position of being up at bat, I would grip my weapon between sweaty little hands, gaze at the pitcher with eyes that begged for mercy...then flail wildly at the object speeding toward my head.

Athlete of the Month, I was not.

And yet, when a friend suggested that my next romance center around a baseball setting, I found that I could not resist. Hopes. Dreams. Passion. Devotion. Even a bench-warmer like me knew that I was looking at the perfect ingredients for a romance.

More important to me than the setting, however, are the story's key issues—which once again hit close to home. Like Casey, I battle against bitterness toward people who have treated me unkindly or disrespectfully. Like Tucker, I can obsess about my desire to succeed.

Most of all, I identify with Casey's need to take her anger to God. When I feel doubt or frustration, I often turn away—try to hide my face. But God knows my heart. I cannot conceal my struggles from him. In recent months, a dear friend, Kari Lundberg, helped me to discover great hope in Isaiah 43:26. "'Who has a case against Me?'" God says. "'Let him draw near to Me.'" And so, I am slowly learning to turn to him—even with the hard, ugly stuff that's deep inside.

What are the doubts, questions, and anger you're wrestling with today? Are you embarrassed, ashamed to take them to God? Or are you drawing near to him?

Believe me, I know: it's hard to do. Terrifying, even.

And yet, in the face of life's toughest issues and feelings, I can't imagine a safer place to be.

Write to Shari MacDonald
c/o Palisades
P.O. Box 1720
Sisters, Oregon 97759